The White Stripes
ELEPHANT

Transcribed by Steve Gorenberg

Album artwork by The Third Man
Album layout by Bruce Brand at Arthole
White Stripes photography by Patrick Pantano

ISBN 978-1-57560-681-1

Visit our website at www.cherrylane.com

Contents

SEVEN NATION ARMY

Words and Music by
Jack White

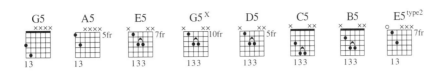

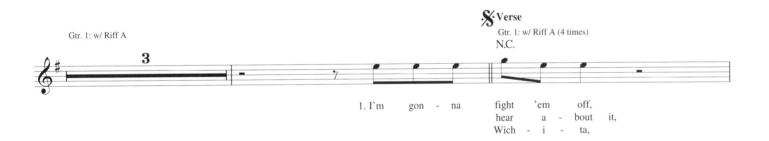

Back and forth through my ___ mind ___
And that ain't what you want to ___ hear,
All the words are gon-na bleed from ___ me ___

___ be - hind a cig - a - rette. ___
___ but that's what I'll ___ do. ___
___ and I will think no ___ more. ___

And the
And the
And the

Interlude

To Coda 1 ⊕
To Coda 2 ⊕

G5   A5   E5   G5ˣ E5 D5

Rhy. Fig. 1   End Rhy. Fig. 1   Rhy. Fig. 2

Gtr. 2
(dist.)

mf   *f*

mes - sage com - ing from my ___ eyes ___ says leave it a - lone. ___
feel - ing com - ing from my ___ bones ___ says find a home. ___
stains com - ing from my ___ blood tell me go back ___ home. ___

Gtr. 3
(dist.)

Rhy. Fig. 1A   End Rhy. Fig. 1A   Rhy. Fig. 2A

mf   *f*
                                        w/ slide

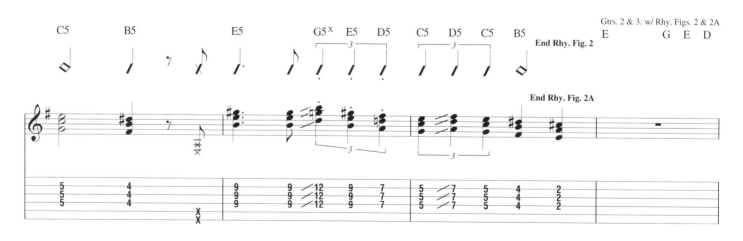

Gtrs. 2 & 3: w/ Rhy. Figs. 2 & 2A

C5   B5   E5   G5ˣ E5 D5   C5 D5 C5 B5   E   G E D

End Rhy. Fig. 2

End Rhy. Fig. 2A

Gtrs. 2 & 3: w/ Rhy. Figs. 1 & 1A

C   B   E   G E D C D C B   A/B   G5

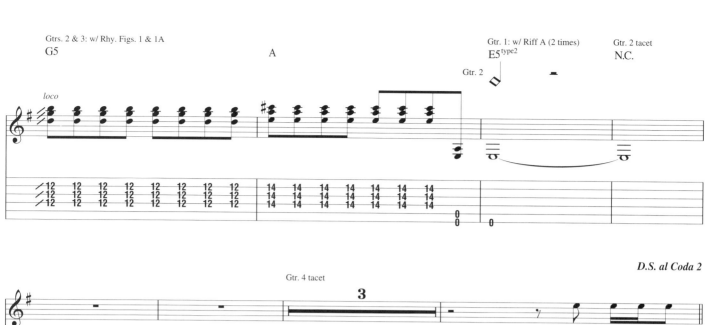

D.S. al Coda 2

3. I'm go - ing to

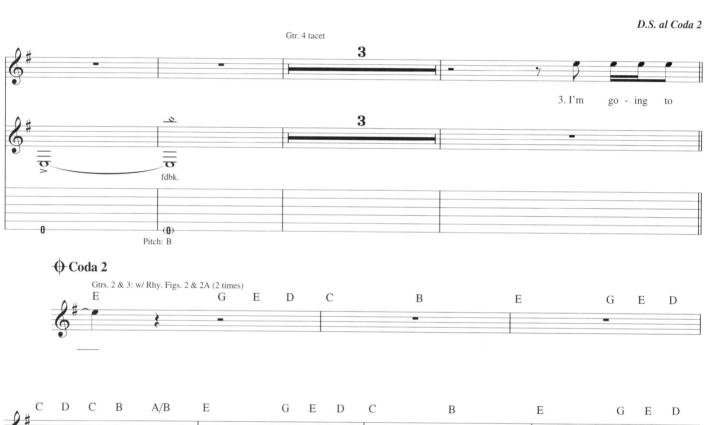

⊕ Coda 2

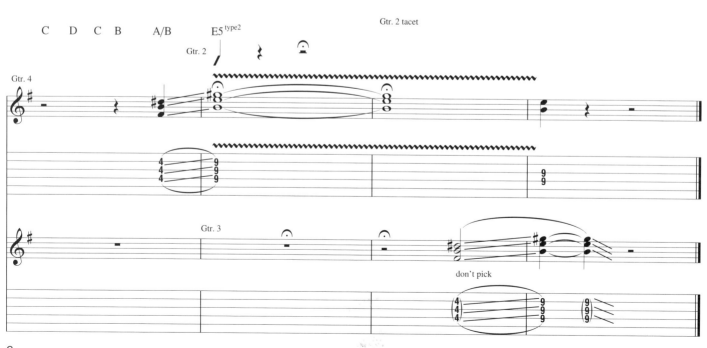

BLACK MATH

Words and Music by
Jack White

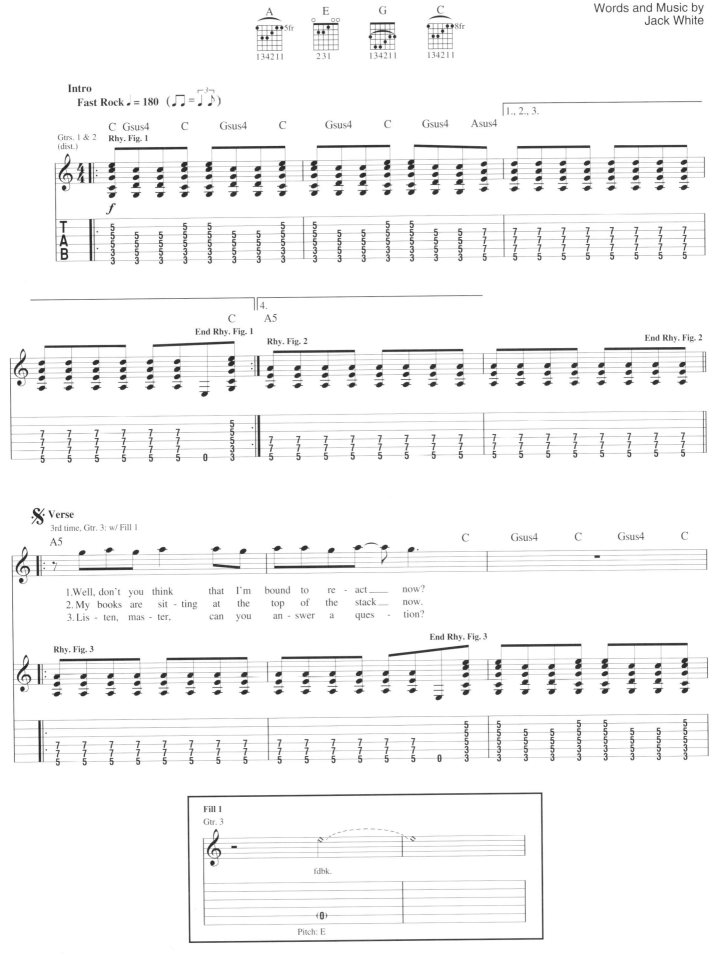

1. Well, don't you think that I'm bound to re - act ___ now?
2. My books are sit - ting at the top of the stack ___ now.
3. Lis - ten, mas - ter, can you an - swer a ques - tion?

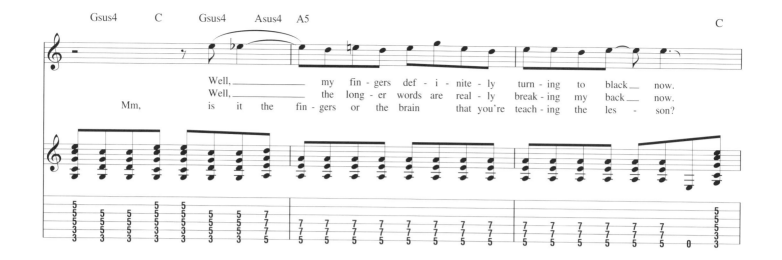

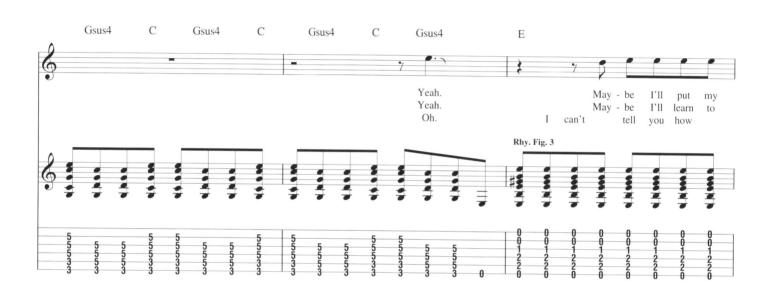

*Flick toggle switch on and off in rhythm indicated.

9

THERE'S NO HOME FOR YOU HERE

Words and Music by
Jack White

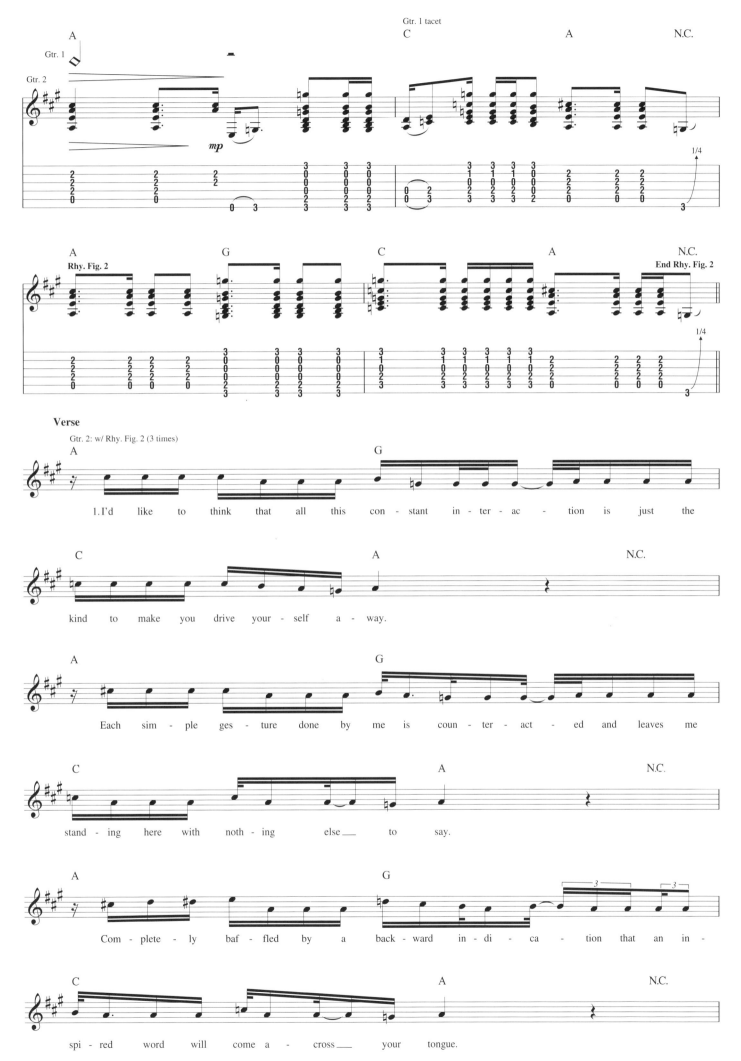

Hands mov - ing up - ward to pro - pel the sit - u - a - tion have sim - ply

halt - ed, now the con - ver - sa - tion's done.

Chorus

Gtrs. 1 & 2: w/ Rhy. Fig. 1

There's no home for you here, girl; go a - way. There's no home for you here.

Gtr. 1 tacet

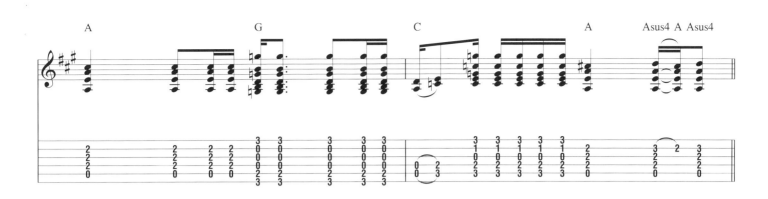

Verse

Gtr. 2: w/ Rhy. Fig. 2 (3 times)

2. I'm on - ly wait - ing for the prop - er time to tell you that it's im - pos - si - ble to get a - long with you.

It's hard to look you in the face when we are talk - ing, so it helps to have a mir - ror in the room.

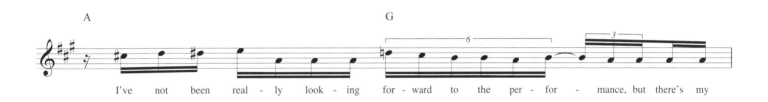

I've not been real - ly look - ing for - ward to the per - for - mance, but there's my

cue and there's a ques - tion on your face.

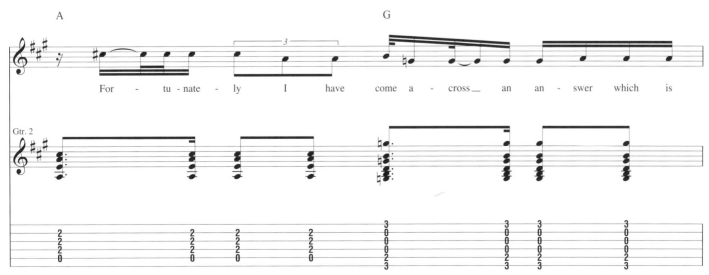

For - tu - nate - ly I have come a - cross an an - swer which is

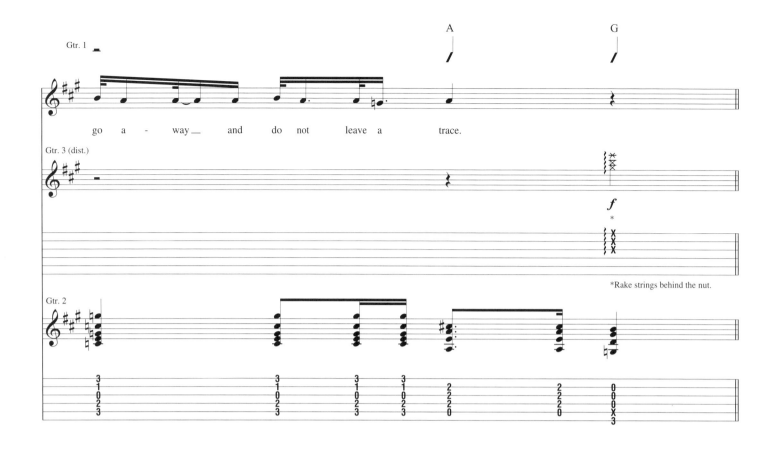

go a - way ___ and do not leave a trace.

*Rake strings behind the nut.

Interlude

Gtrs. 1 & 2 tacet

N.C.(A)

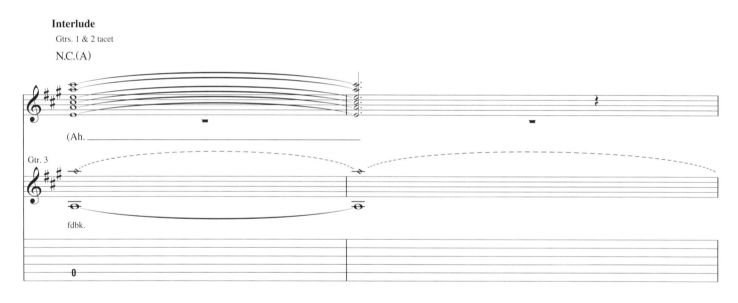

(Ah. ___

fdbk.

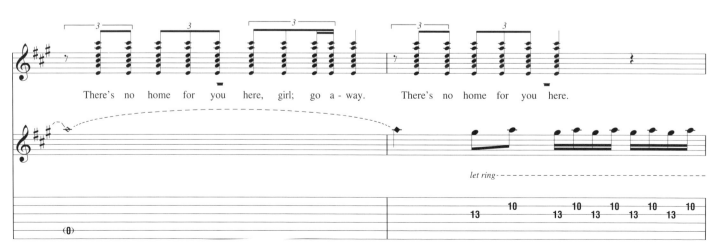

There's no home for you here, girl; go a - way. There's no home for you here.

let ring -

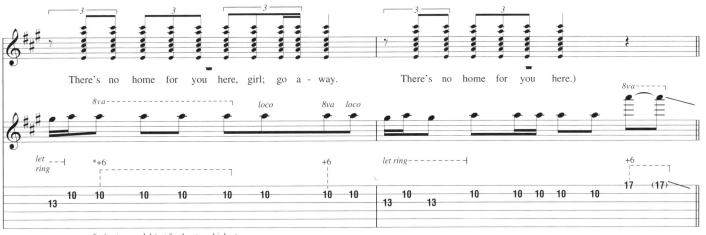

There's no home for you here, girl; go a - way.   There's no home for you here.)

*w/ octave pedal (set for 1 octave higher)

Guitar Solo

Gtrs. 1 & 2: w/ Rhy. Fig. 1 (2 times)

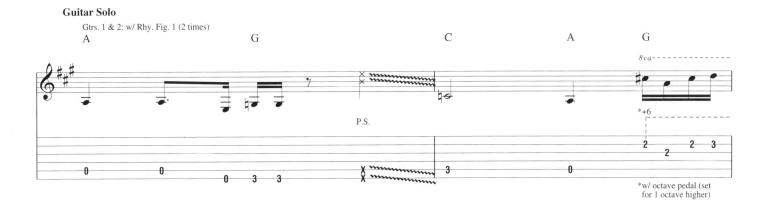

*w/ octave pedal (set for 1 octave higher)

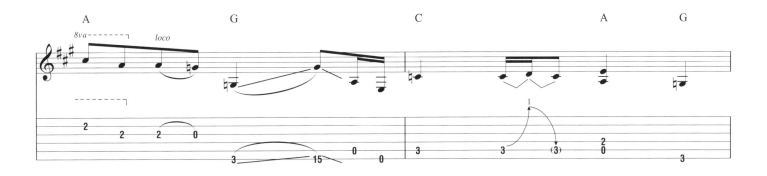

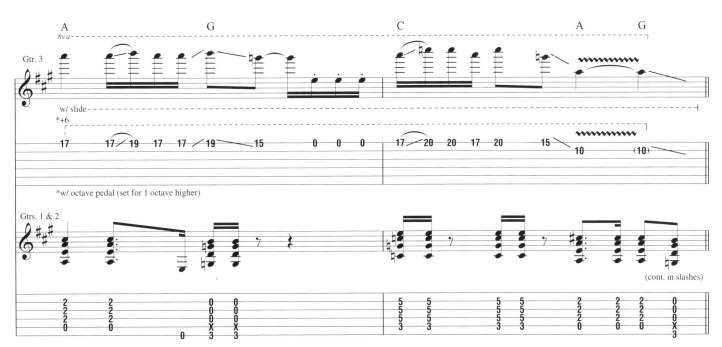

(cont. in slashes)

Waking up for break-fast. Burn-ing match-es. Talk-ing quick-ly. Break-ing bau-bles. Throw-ing gar-bage. Drink-ing so-da. Look-ing hap-py. Tak-ing pic-tures. So com-plete-ly stu-pid. Just go a-way.

(Ah.)

There's no home for you here, girl; go a-way. There's no home for you here.

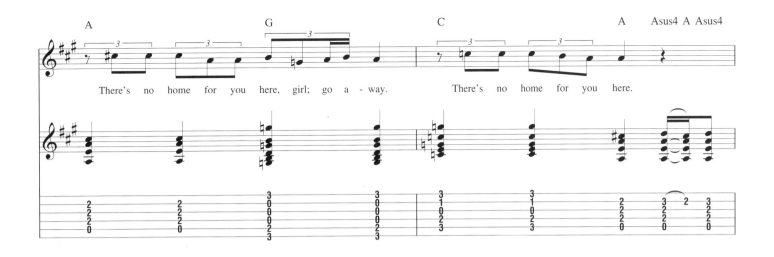

There's no home for you here, girl; go a - way.   There's no home for you here.

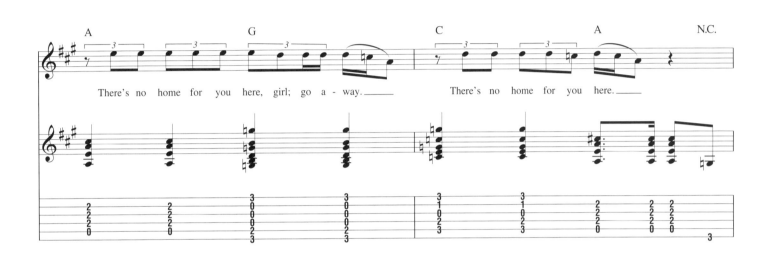

There's no home for you here, girl; go a - way.____   There's no home for you here.____

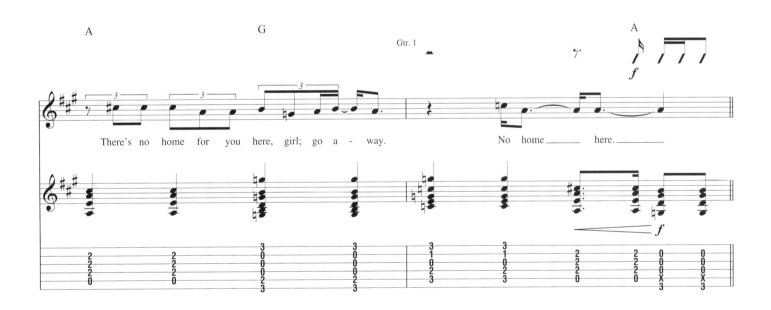

There's no home for you here, girl; go a - way.   No home____ here.____

Outro

Gtrs. 1 & 2: w/ Rhy. Fig. 1

Repeat and fade

There's no home for you here, girl; go a - way.   There's no home for you here.

I JUST DON'T
WHAT TO DO WITH MYSELF

Lyric by Hal David
Music by Burt Bacharach

Bridge

needs the sun and rain,

I need your

sweet love to be loved a - way.

3. Well, I don't

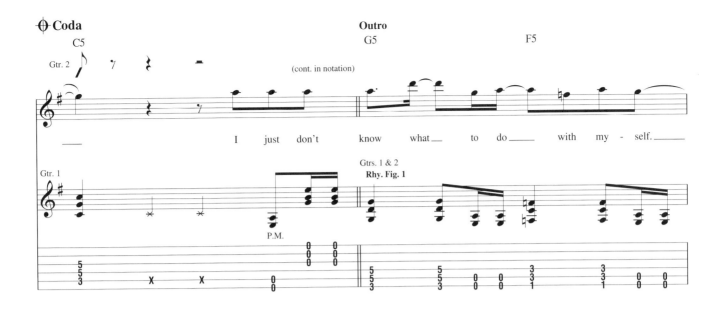

I just don't know what to do with my-self.

Just don't know what to do with my-self.

Just don't know what to do with my-self. I don't

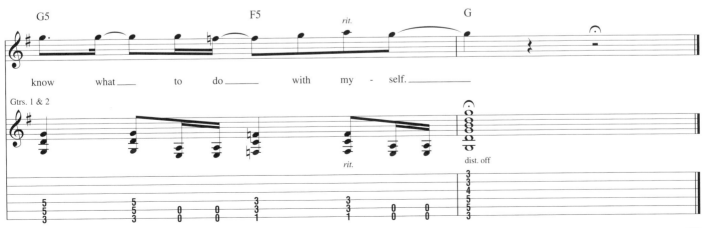

know what to do with my-self.

IN THE COLD, COLD NIGHT

Words and Music by
Jack White

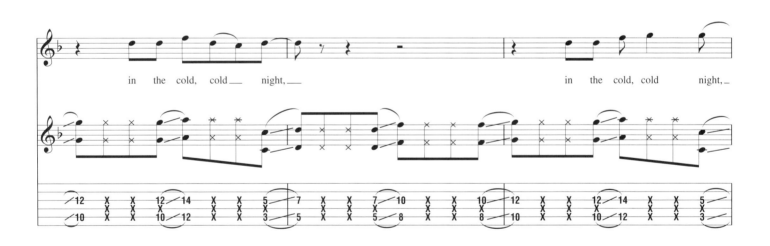

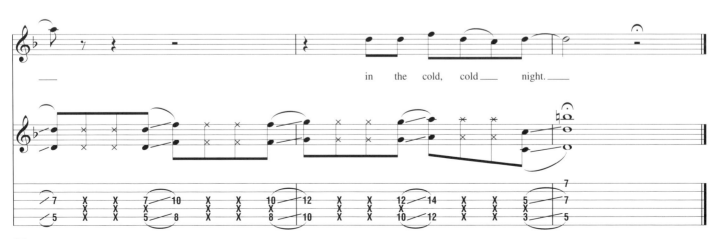

I WANT TO BE THE BOY TO WARM YOUR MOTHER'S HEART

Words and Music by
Jack White

Gtr. 2: Open G tuning:
(low to high) D-G-D-G-B-D

Verse

Moderately slow ♩ = 74

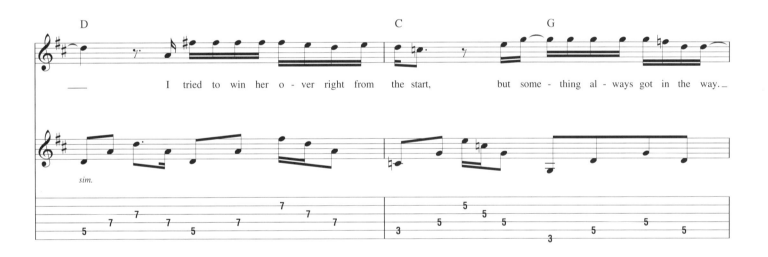

1. I want to be the boy___ to warm your moth-er's heart. I'm so scared to take___ you a-way.___

Gtr. 1 (semi-clean)

mf

let ring

*Chord symbols reflect overall harmony.

___ I tried to win her o-ver right from the start, but some-thing al-ways got in the way.___

sim.

___ We've been sit-ting in your back-yard for hours, but she won't e-ven come out and say hi,___

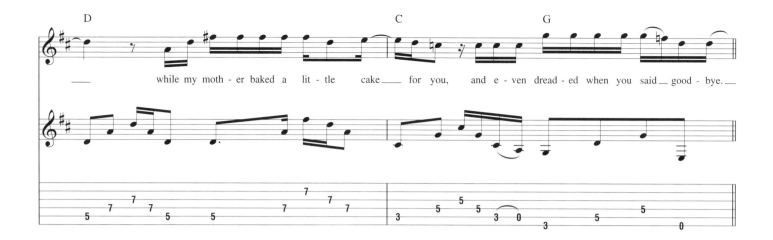

while my moth-er baked a lit-tle cake___ for you, and e-ven dread-ed when you said___ good-bye.___

𝄋 Chorus

2nd time, Gtr. 2: w/ Fill 1

What kind of cart-wheels do I have__ to pull?___ What kind of joke should I lay on her now?__

P.M.

*On D.S., vocal substitutes 1/4 rest for beat 1.

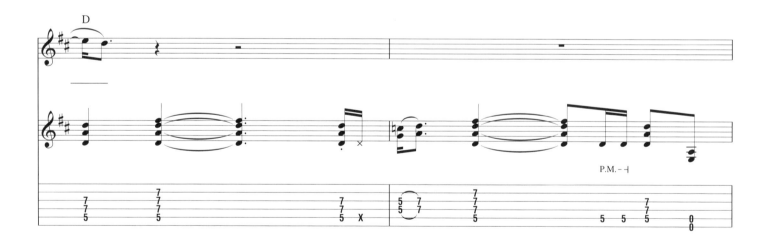

P.M. - ⌐

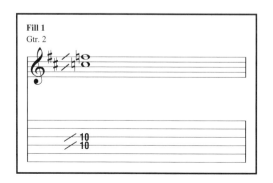

Fill 1
Gtr. 2

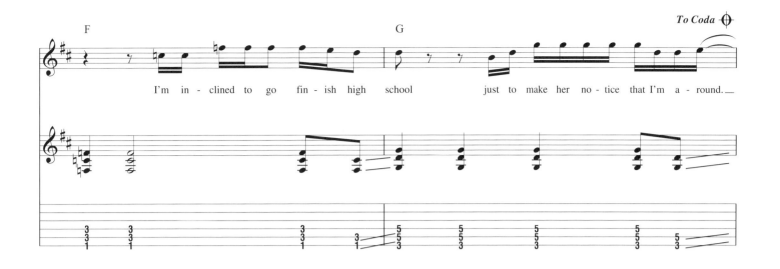

I'm in - clined to go fin - ish high school just to make her no - tice that I'm a - round.

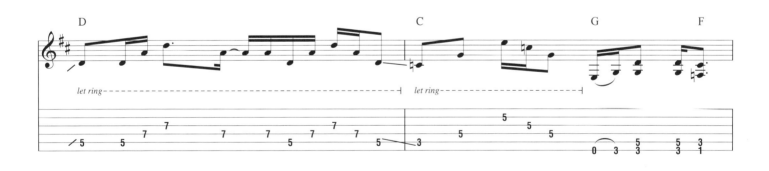

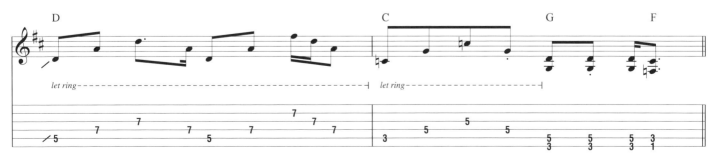

Verse

2. Well, noth-ing I come up with seems___ to work, feels like ev-'ry-thing I say is a lie.___

And nev-er have I felt like such___ a jerk, I'm a-fraid to e-ven o-pen my eyes.___

Be-cause I real-ly don't want her to judge___ me, I want her to real-ly know who I am.___

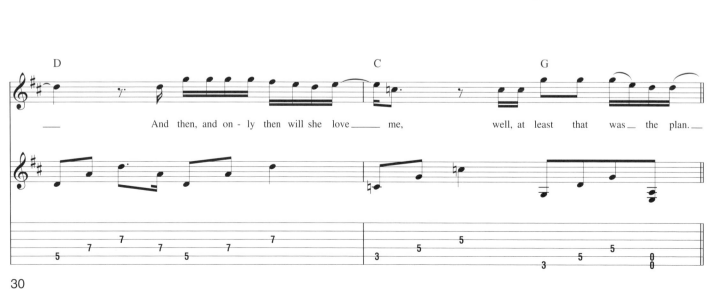

And then, and on-ly then will she love___ me, well, at least that was___ the plan.___

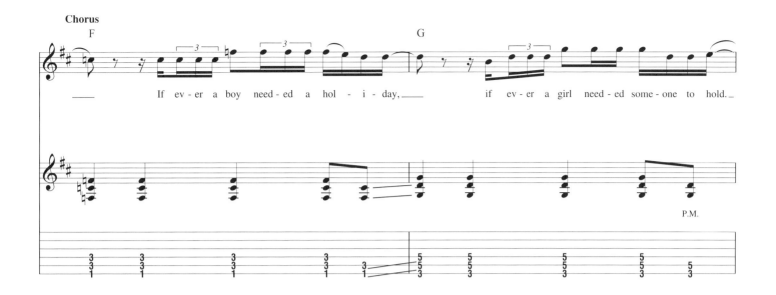

If ev-er a boy need-ed a hol-i-day,___ if ev-er a girl need-ed some-one to hold._

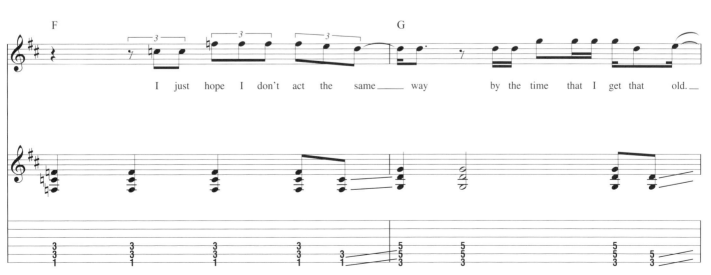

I just hope I don't act the same___ way by the time that I get that old. __

Guitar Solo

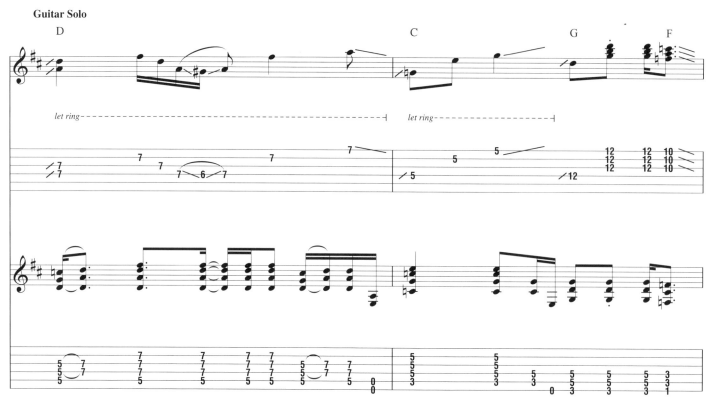

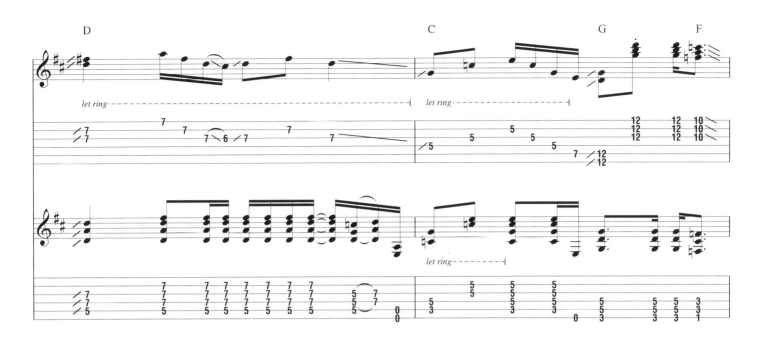

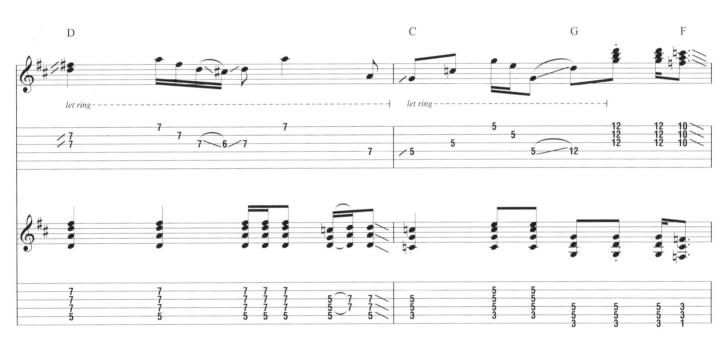

D.S. al Coda

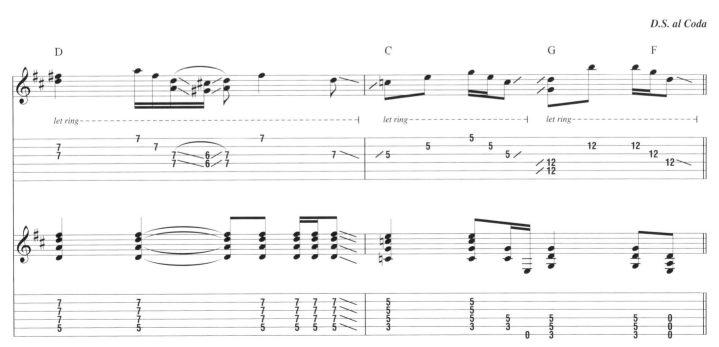

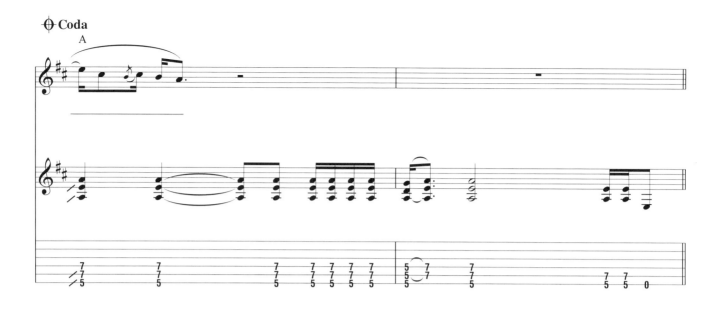

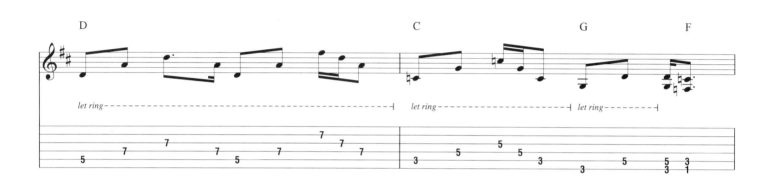

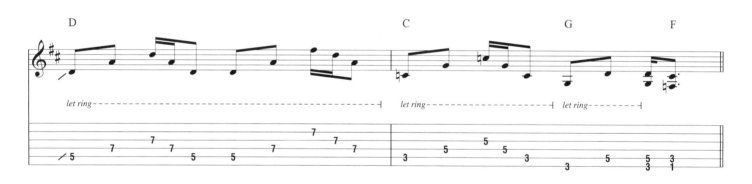

Verse

3. I nev-er said I was the heir to a for - tune, I nev-er claimed to have_ an - y looks._

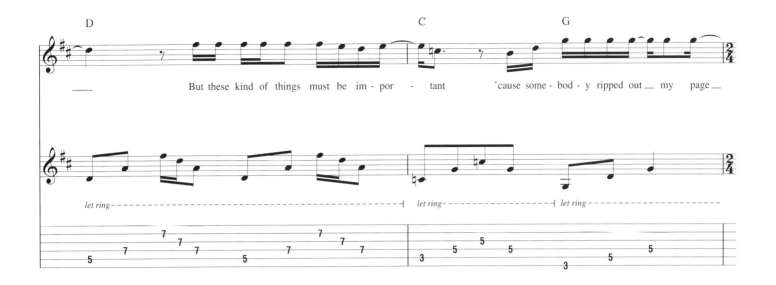

But these kind of things must be im - por - tant 'cause some - bod - y ripped out __ my page __

__ in your tel - e - phone book. _____

I want to warm her heart.

YOU'VE GOT HER IN YOUR POCKET

Words and Music by
Jack White

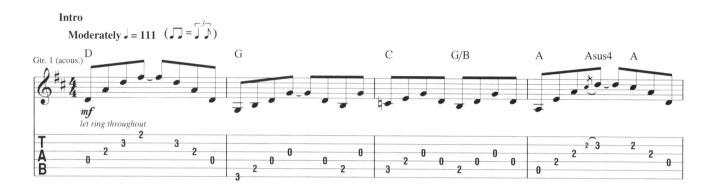

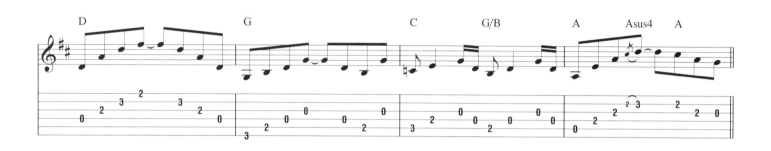

Chorus

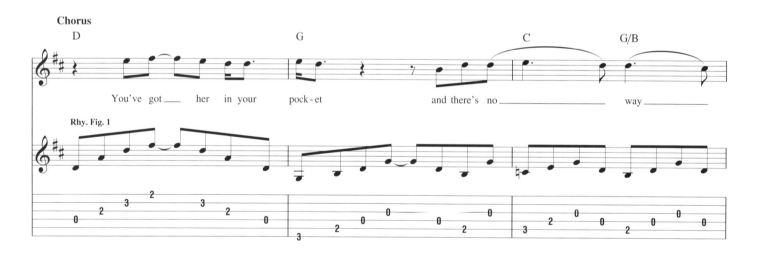

You've got ___ her in your pock-et   and there's no _____ way _____

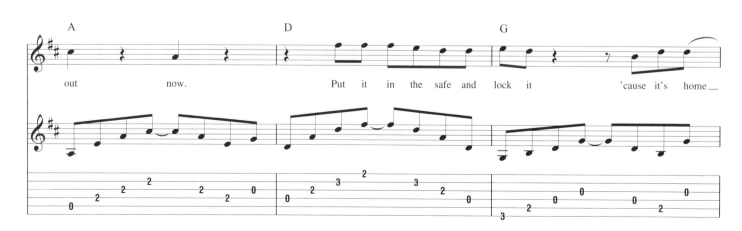

out   now.   Put it in the safe and lock it   'cause it's home __

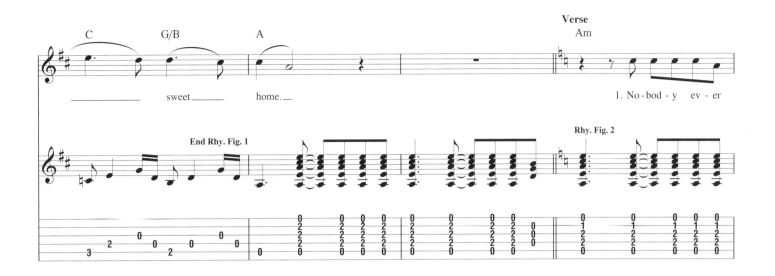

sweet home.　　1. No-bod-y ev-er

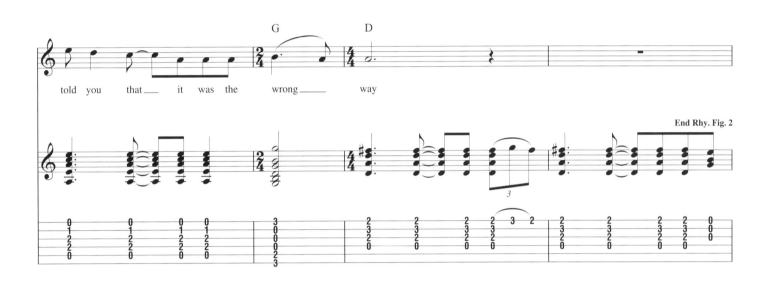

told you that it was the wrong way

to trick a wom-an, make her feel she did it her way.

And you'll be there if she ev-er feels

BALL AND BISCUIT

Words and Music by
Jack White

Intro
Moderate Blues ♩ = 74

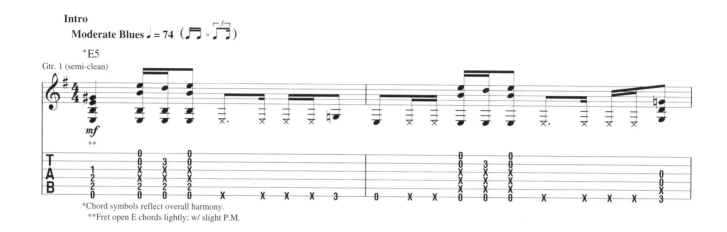

*Chord symbols reflect overall harmony.
**Fret open E chords lightly; w/ slight P.M.

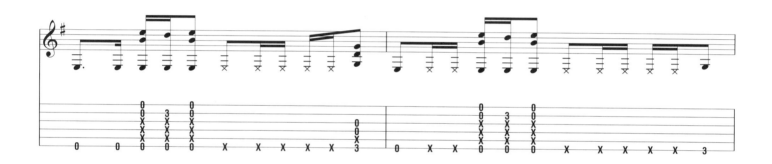

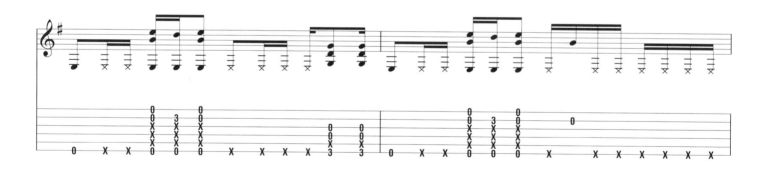

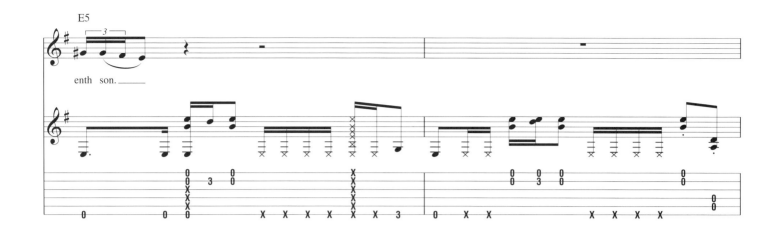

enth son.___

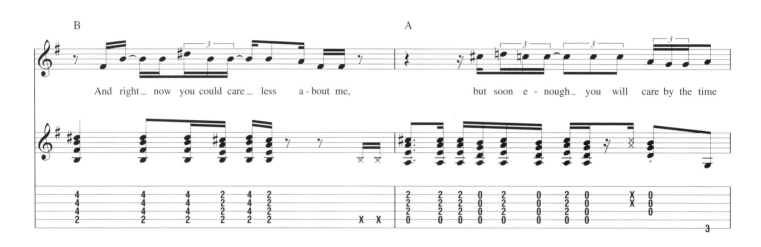

And right___ now you could care___ less a - bout me, but soon e - nough___ you will care by the time

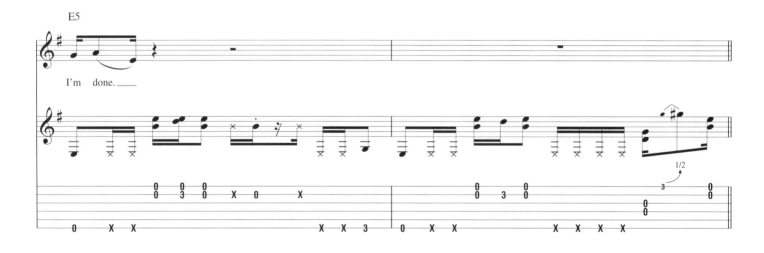

I'm done.___

Chorus

N.C.(E5)

Let's have a ball and a bis - quit, sug - ar, and___ take our sweet lit - tle time___

42

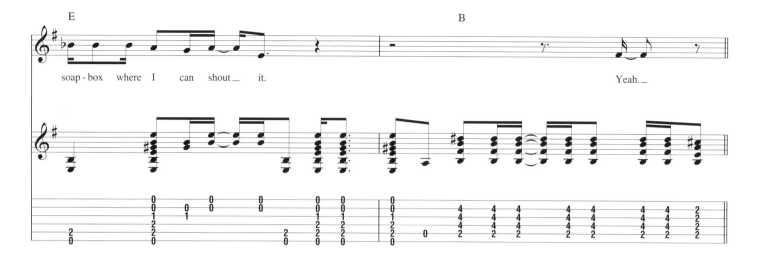

soap - box where I can shout _ it.

Yeah. _

Guitar Solo

E5

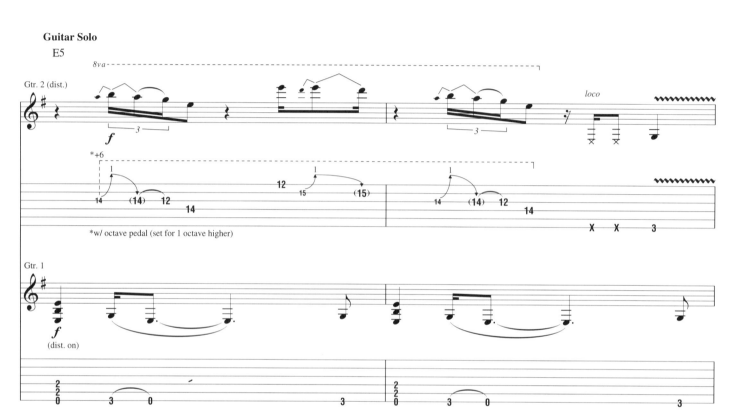

Gtr. 2 (dist.)

*w/ octave pedal (set for 1 octave higher)

Gtr. 1

(dist. on)

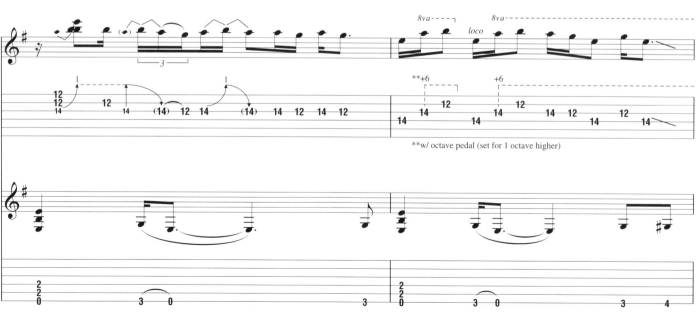

**w/ octave pedal (set for 1 octave higher)

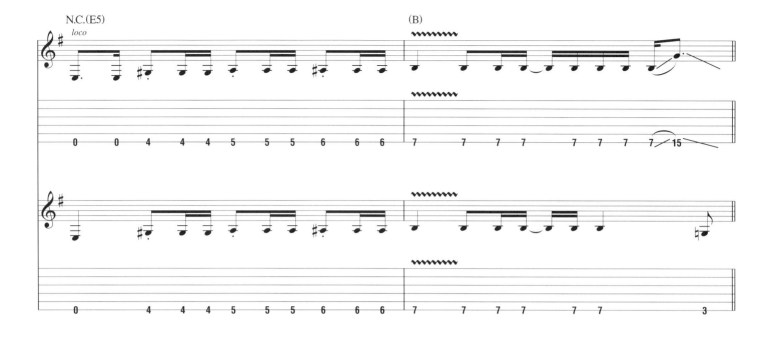

Interlude

Gtr. 2 tacet

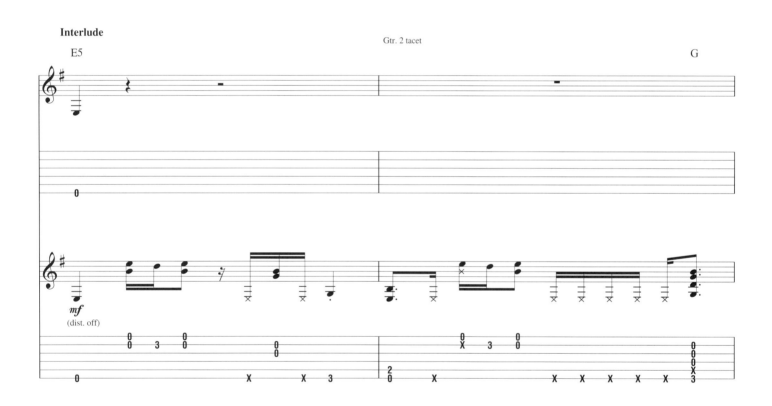

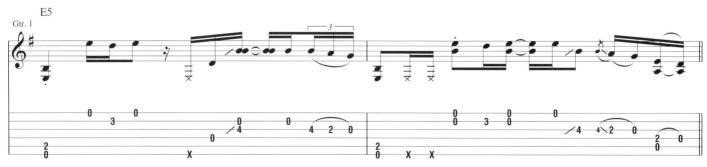

Verse

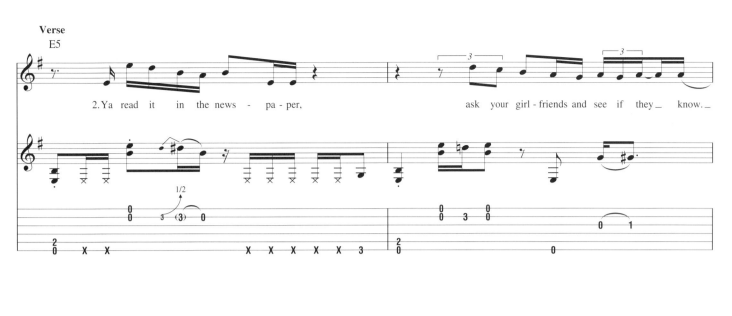

2. Ya read it in the news - pa - per,   ask your girl - friends and see if they_ know._

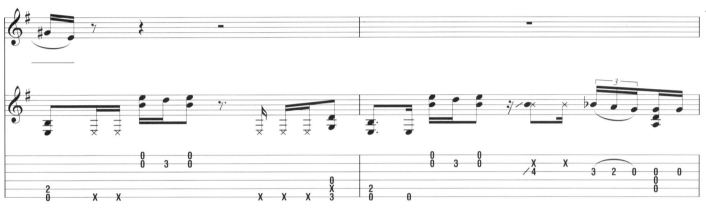

A

Read it in the news - pa - per,   ask your_ girl - friends_ and see if they_

E5

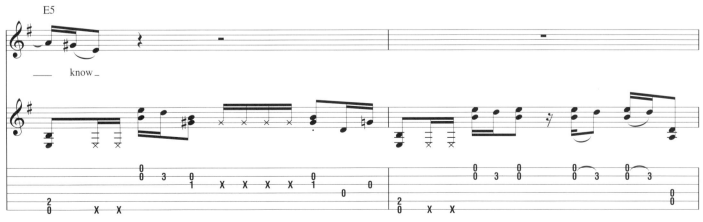

_ know _

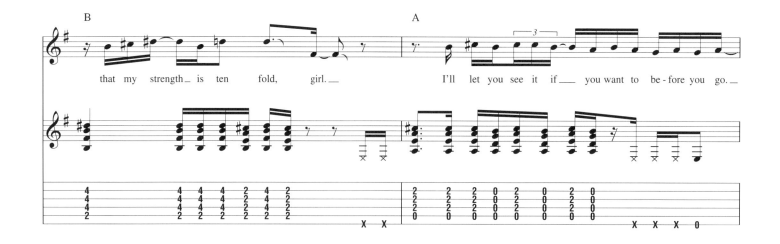

that my strength is ten fold, girl. I'll let you see it if you want to be-fore you go.

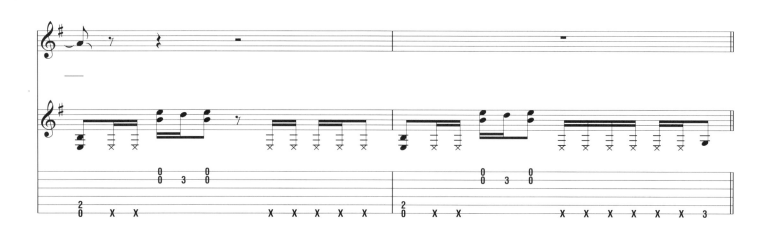

Chorus

N.C.(E5)

Let's have a ball and a bis - quit, sug-ar, and take our sweet lit-tle time

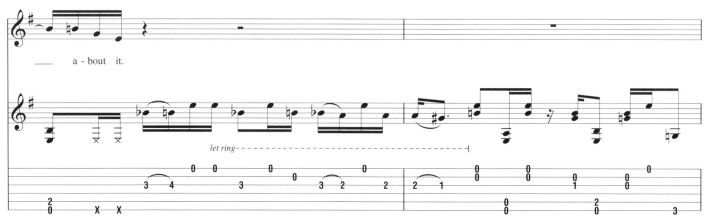

a - bout it.

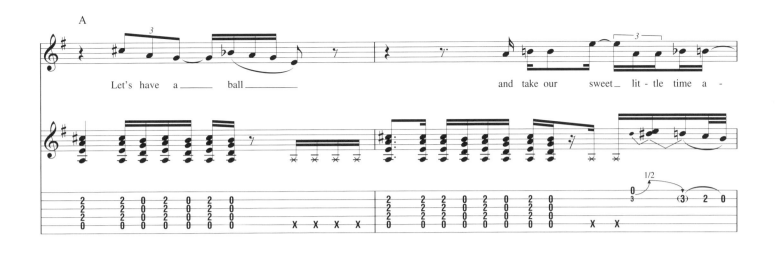

Let's have a _____ ball _____ and take our sweet ___ lit - tle time a -

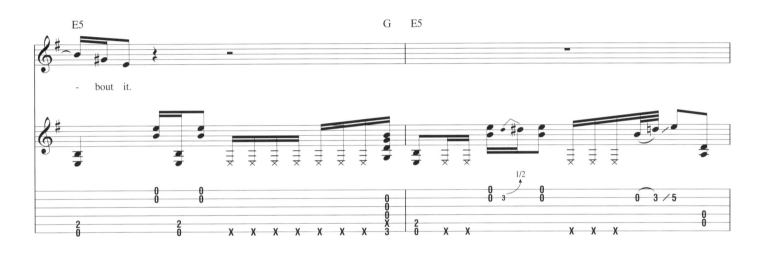

- bout it.

Tell ev -'ry - bod - y in the place___ to just get out, we'll get clean to - geth - er and I'll find me a soap -

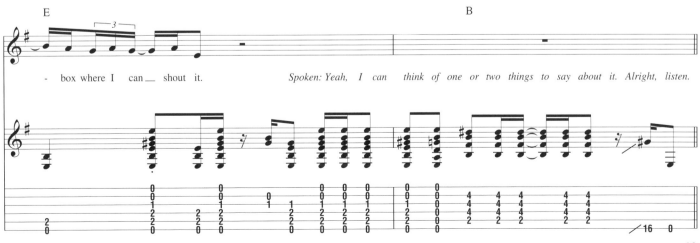

- box where I can___ shout it. *Spoken: Yeah, I can think of one or two things to say about it. Alright, listen.*

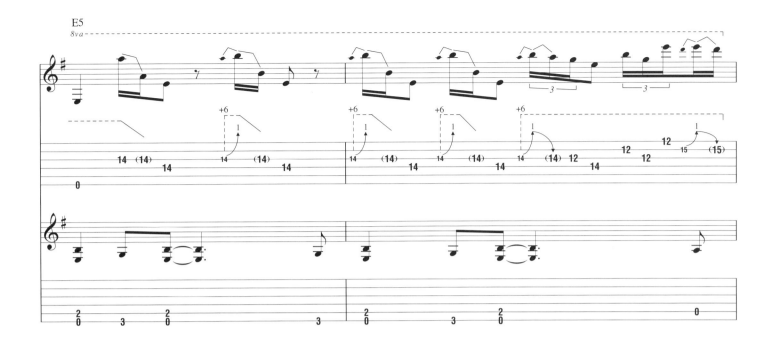

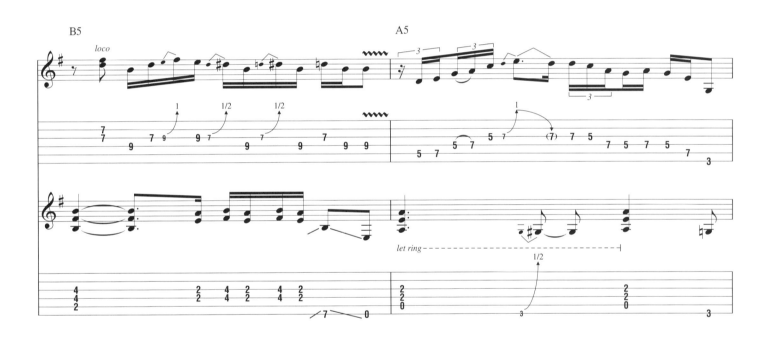

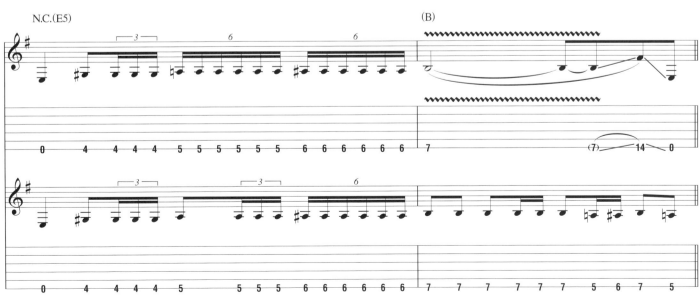

Interlude

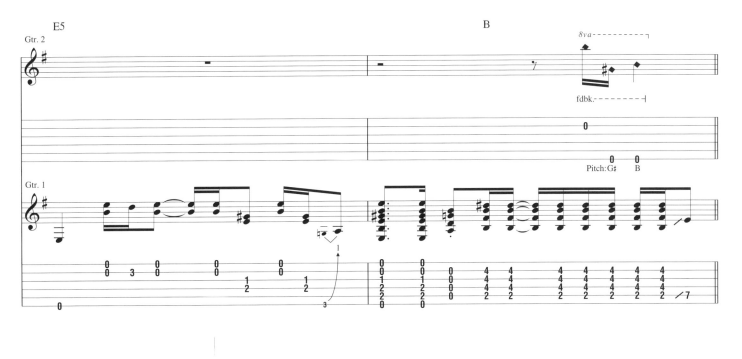

Guitar Solo

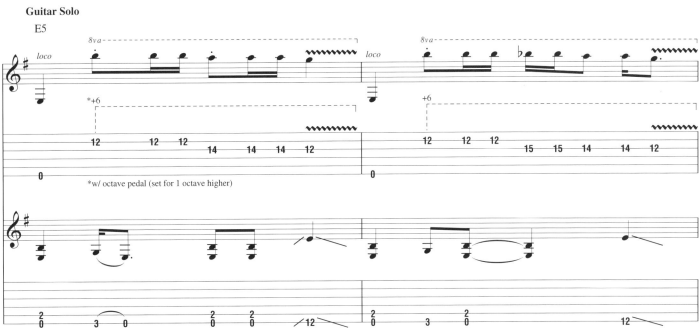

*w/ octave pedal (set for 1 octave higher)

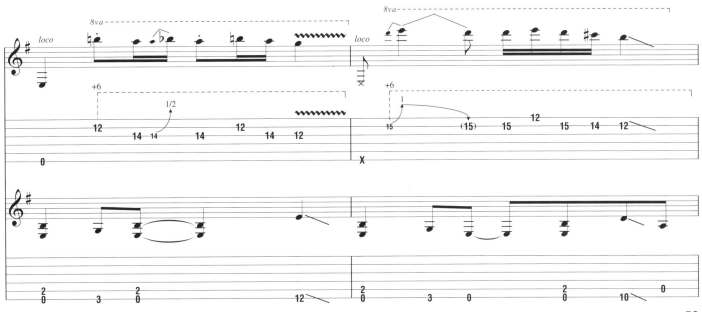

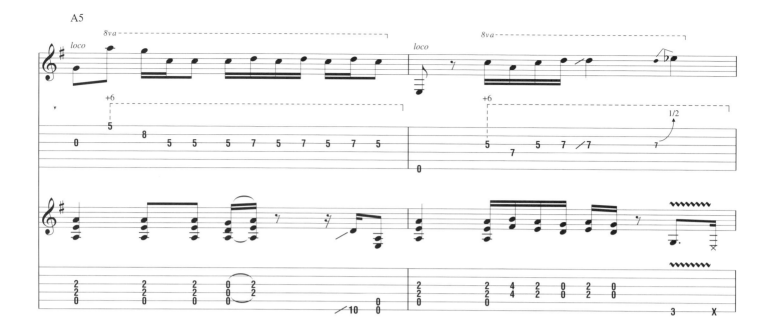

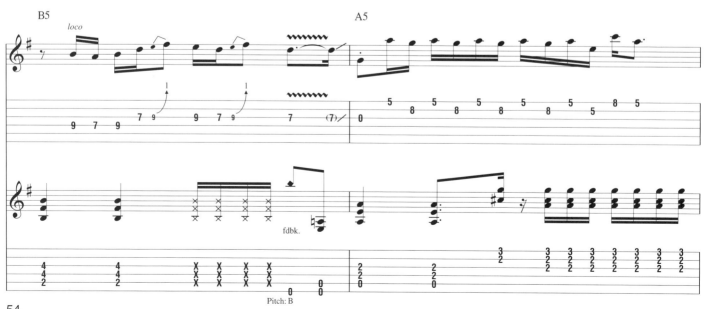

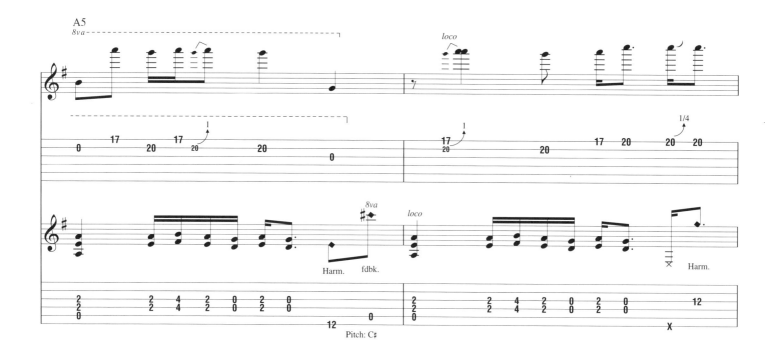

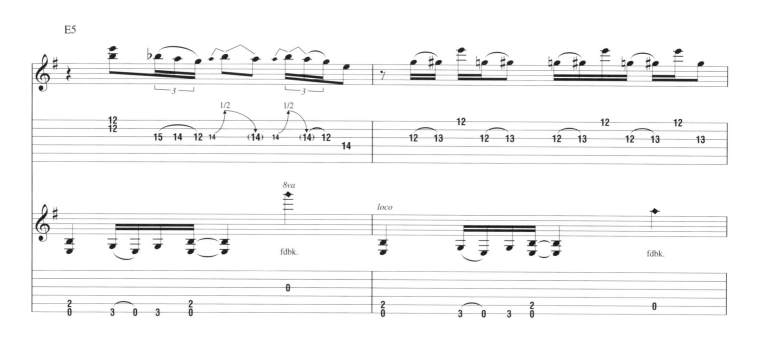

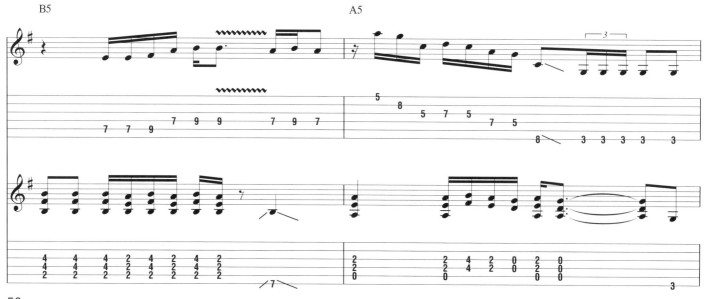

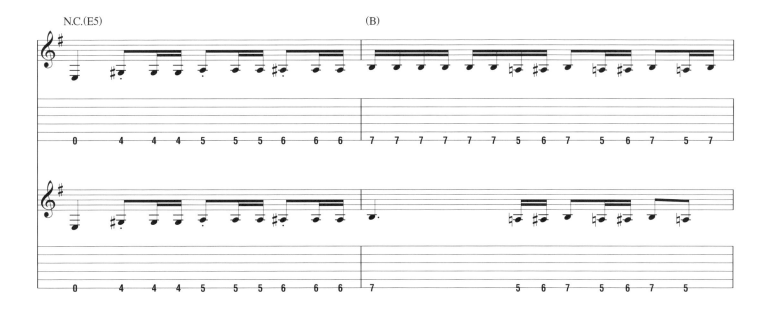

Gtr. 2 tacet

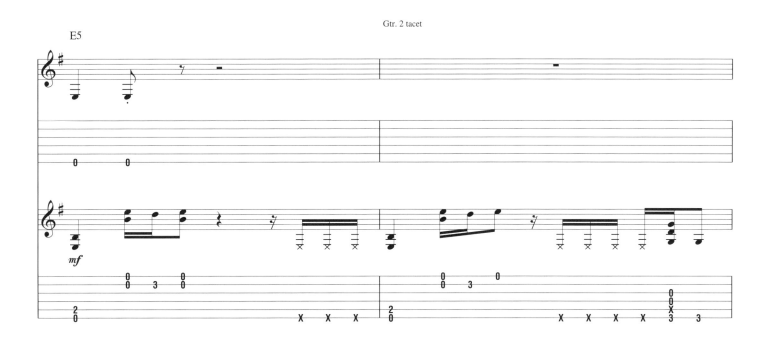

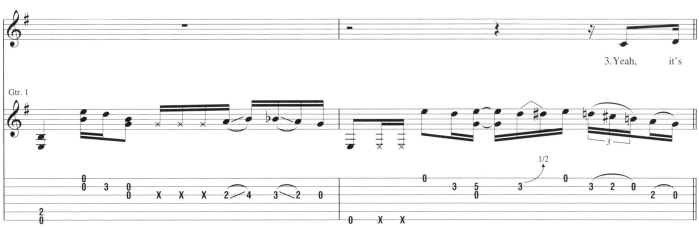

3. Yeah,   it's

Verse

quite   pos - si - ble that I'm your third man,   but it's a fact that I'm the sev - enth son. __

It was the   oth - er two which made me your third,   but it's my __ moth - er who made me the sev - enth __

__ son.

And right now you could care   less a-bout me,

but soon e-nough you will care by the time___

___ I'm   done. ___

Spoken: Yeah, you just wait.

Yeah, stick around,

you'll figure it out.

THE HARDEST BUTTON TO BUTTON

Words and Music by
Jack White

Intro
Moderate Rock ♩ = 128

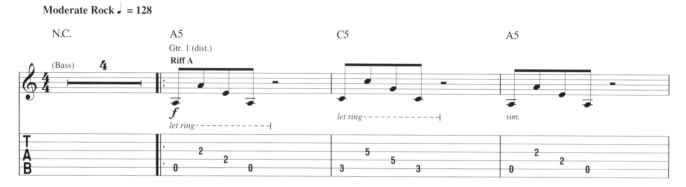

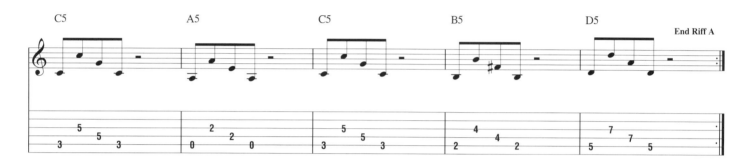

Verse
Gtr. 1: w/ Riff A

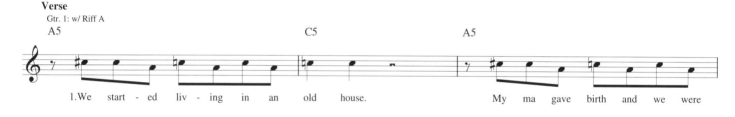

1. We start-ed liv-ing in an old house. My ma gave birth and we were

check-ing it out.___ It was a ba-by boy so we bought him a toy, it was a

ray gun, and it was nine-teen eight-y-one. We named him "Ba-by." He had a

tooth-ache. He start-ed cry-ing, it sound-ed like an earth-quake. It did-n't

LITTLE ACORNS

Words and Music by
Jack White

Intro

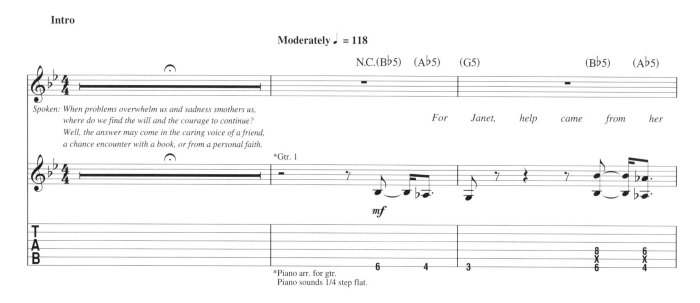

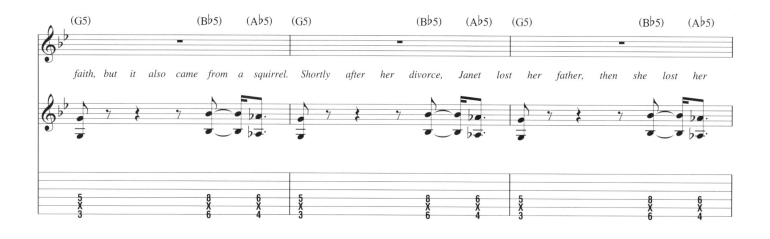

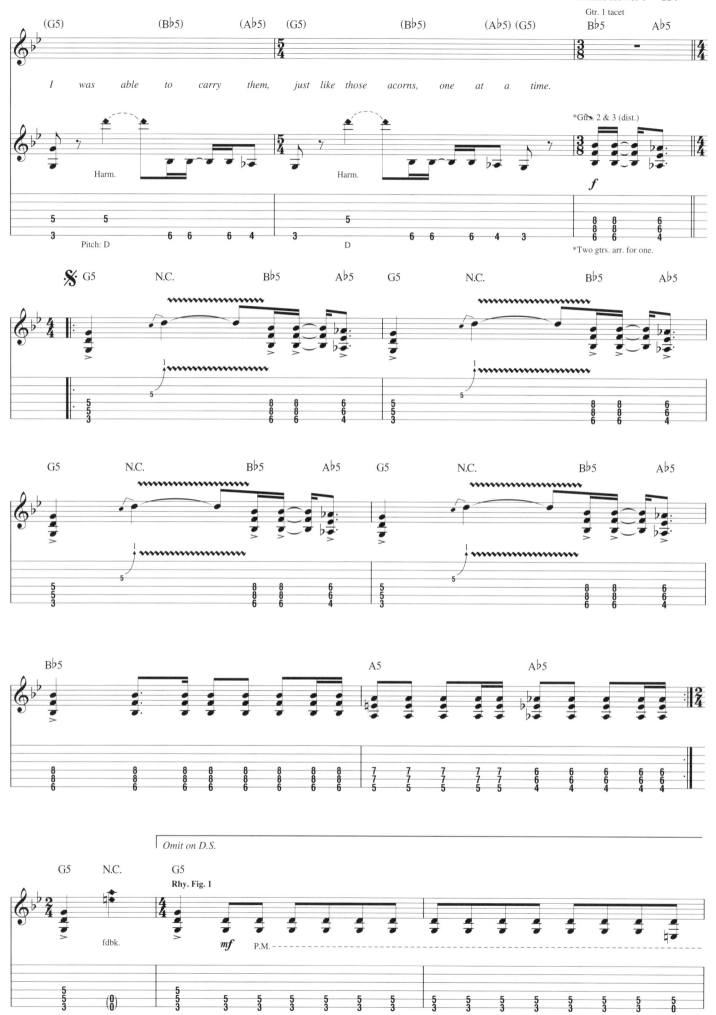

I was able to carry them, just like those acorns, one at a time.

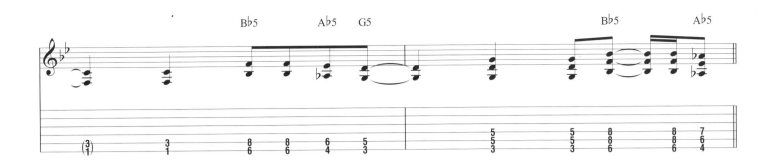

Outro

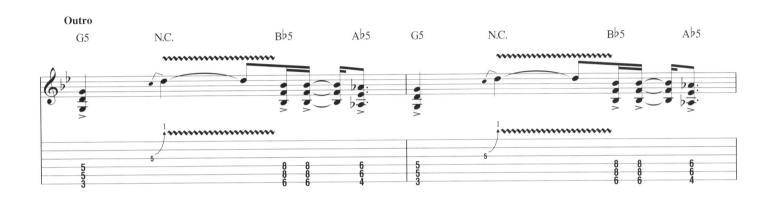

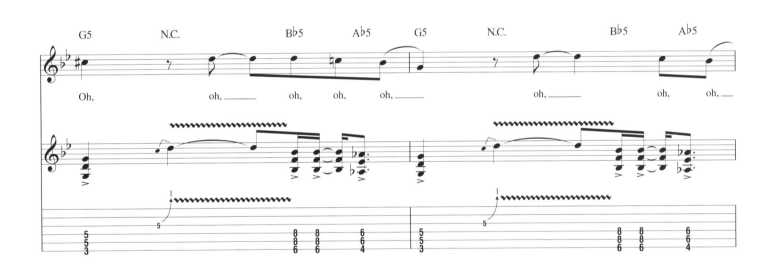

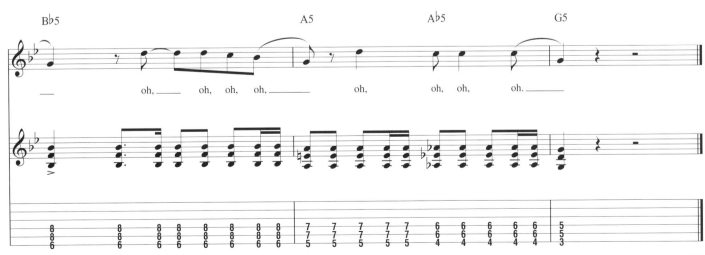

HYPNOTIZE

Words and Music by
Jack White

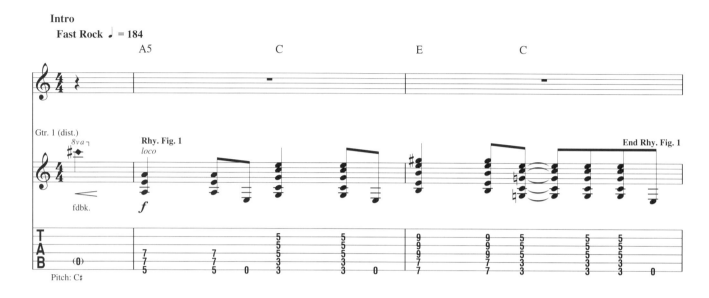

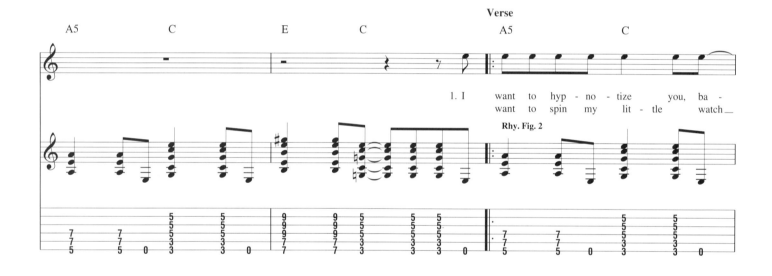

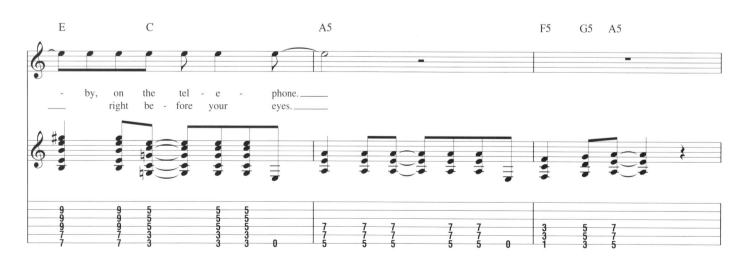

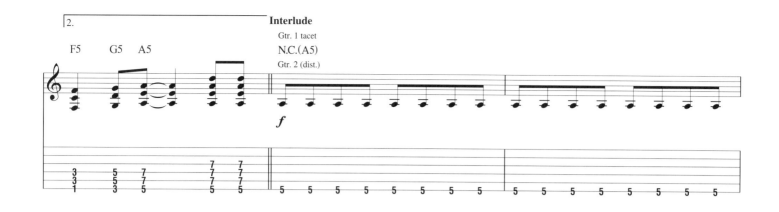

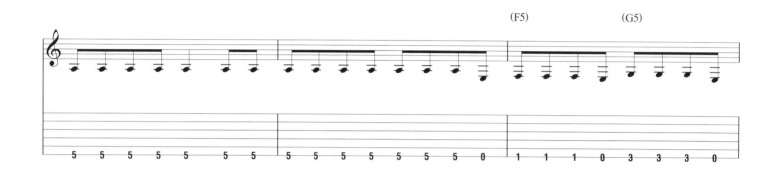

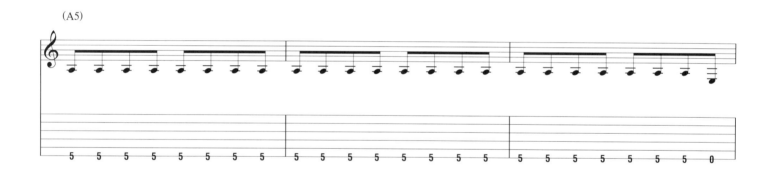

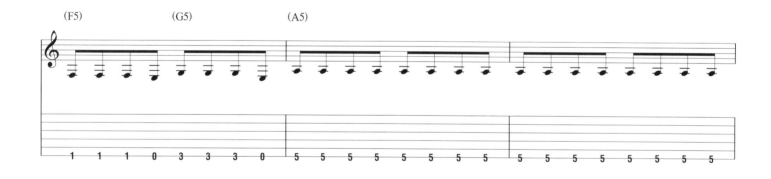

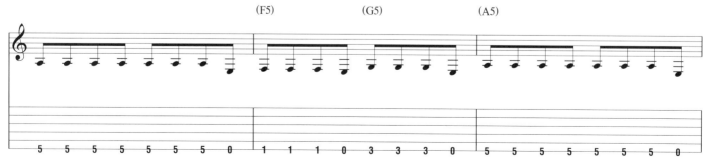

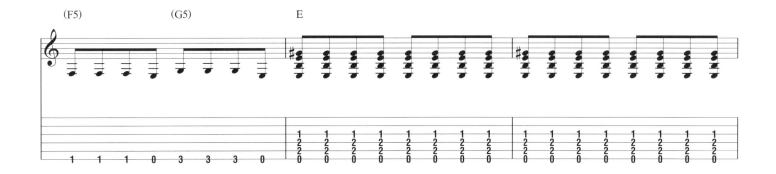

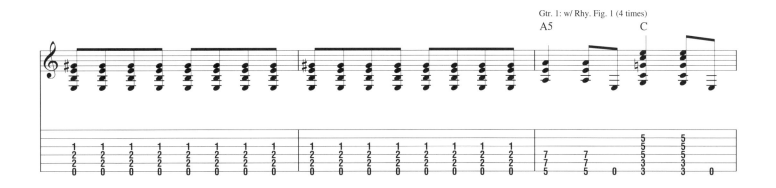

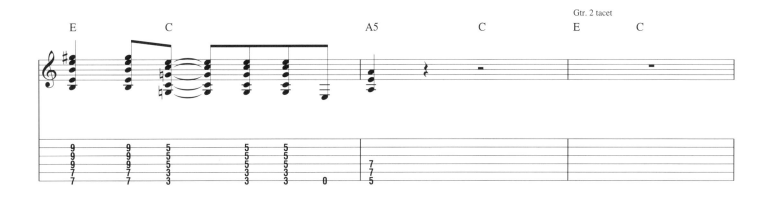

3. I

Verse
Gtr. 1: w/ Rhy. Fig. 2

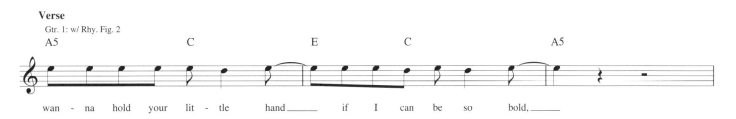

wan - na hold your lit - tle hand_____ if I can be so bold,_____

and be your right hand man till your hand gets old.

And then when all the feel-ing's gone,_____ just de-
cide if you want to keep hold-ing on. I want to hold your lit-tle hand_____
_____ if I can be so bold,_____ if I can be so bold,_____
_____ if I can be so bold._____

Pitch: C#

74

THE AIR NEAR MY FINGERS

Words and Music by
Jack White

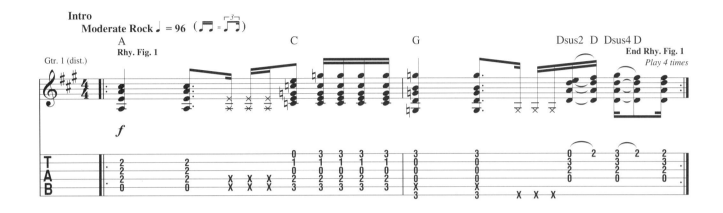

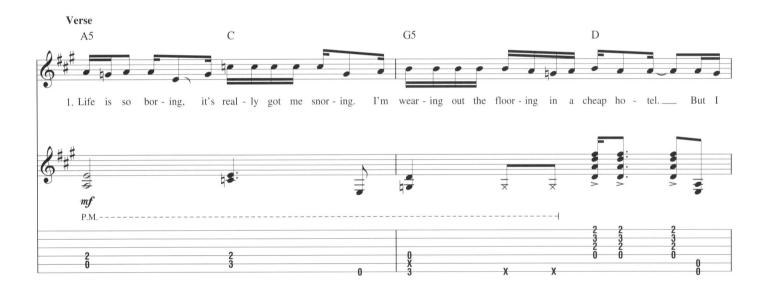

76

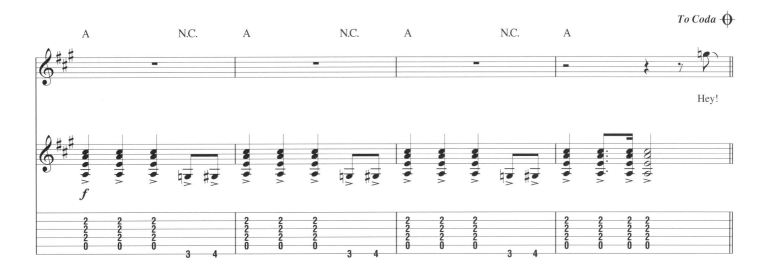

Interlude

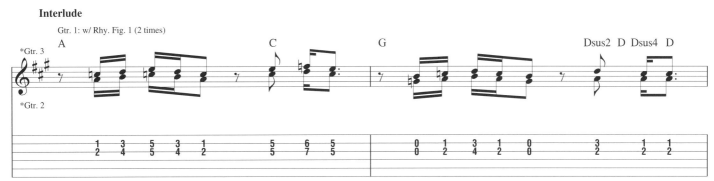

*Keyboards arr. for gtr.

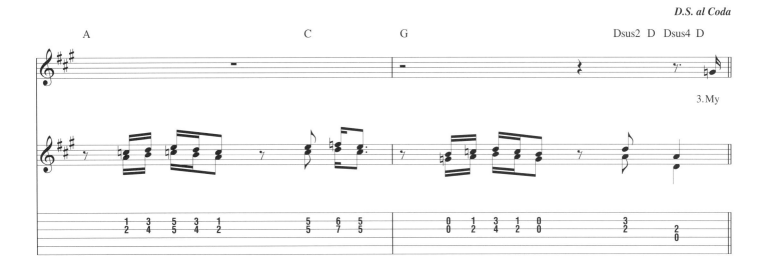

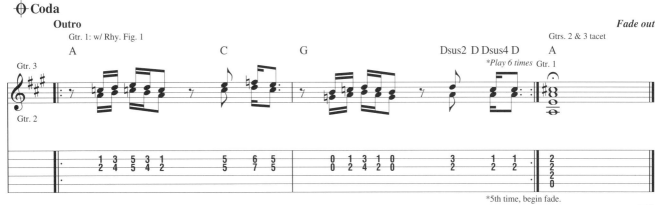

*5th time, begin fade.

GIRL, YOU HAVE NO FAITH IN MEDICINE

Words and Music by
Jack White

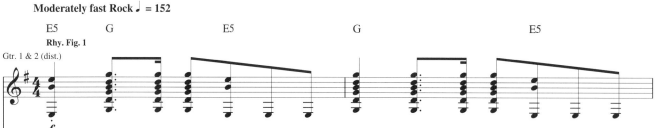

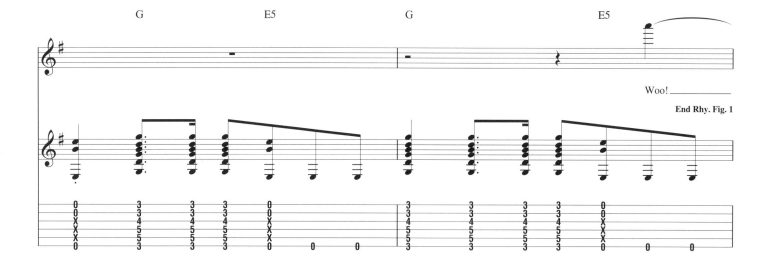

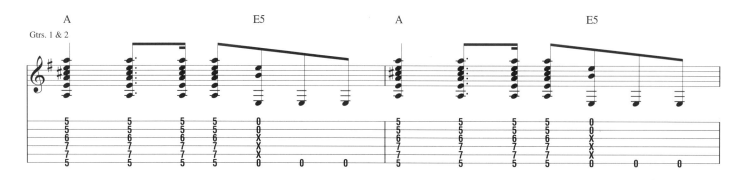

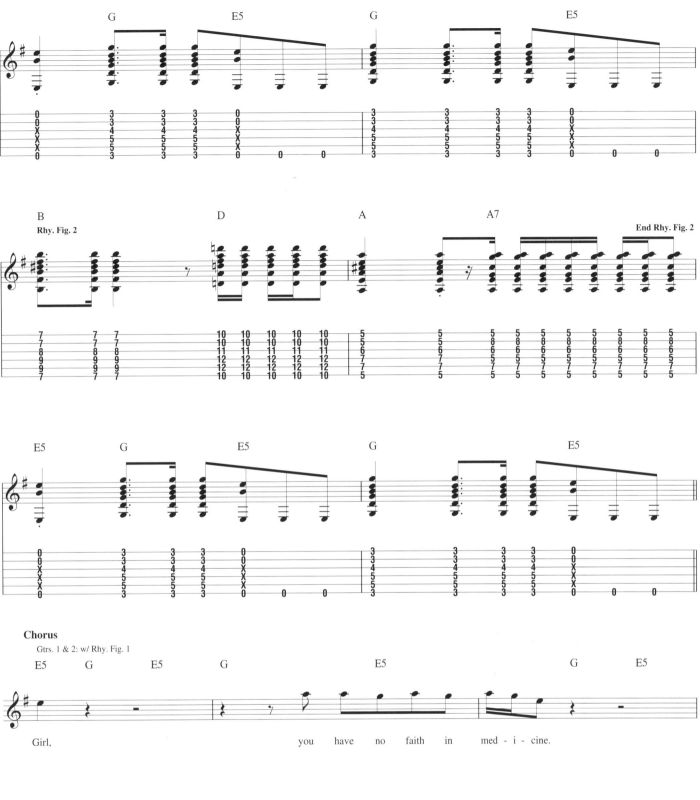

Chorus

Gtrs. 1 & 2: w/ Rhy. Fig. 1

Girl, you have no faith in med - i - cine.

Oh, girl, ____ you have no faith in

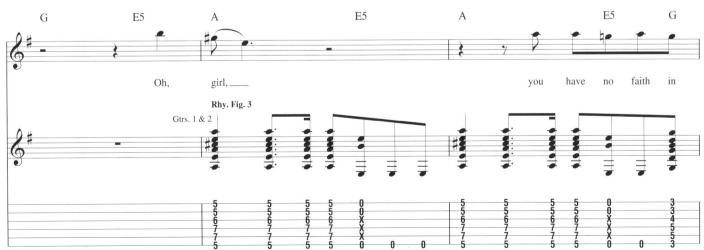

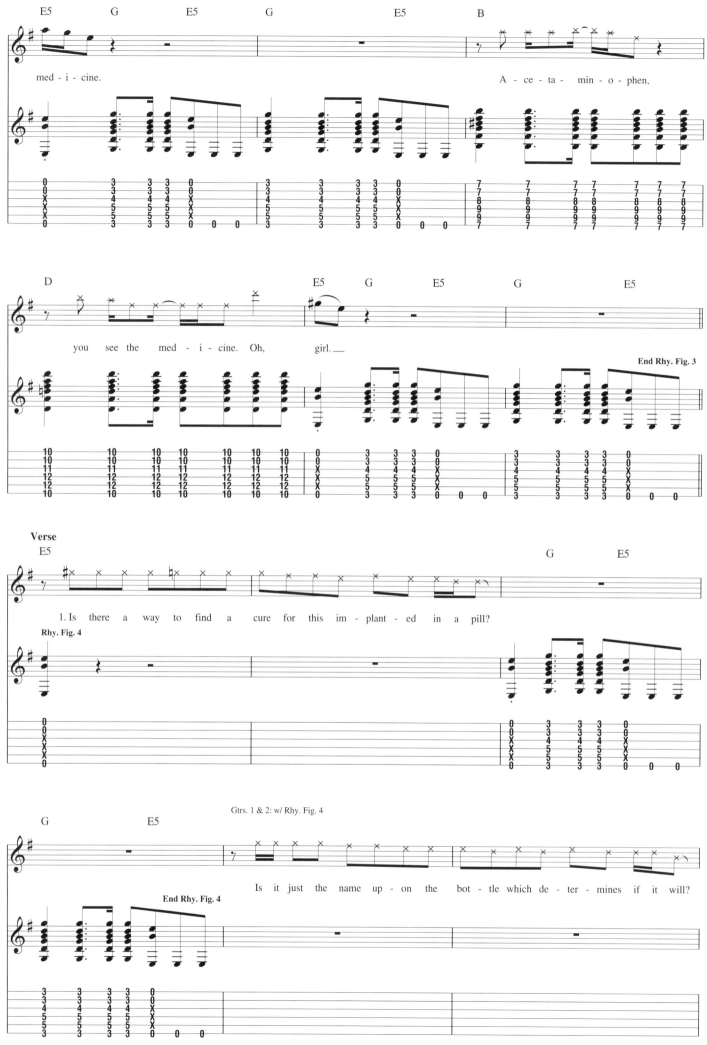

Chorus

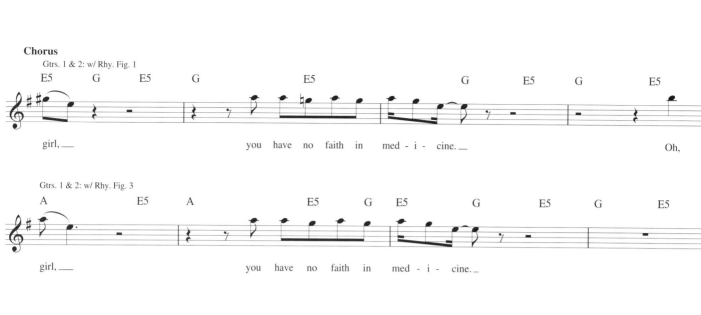

girl, ___   you have no faith in med - i - cine. ___   Oh,

girl, ___   you have no faith in med - i - cine. ___

A - ce - ta - min - o - phen,   you see the med - i - cine. Oh,   girl. ___

Guitar Solo

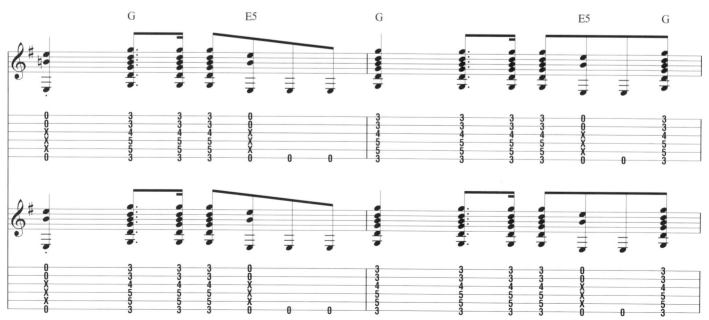

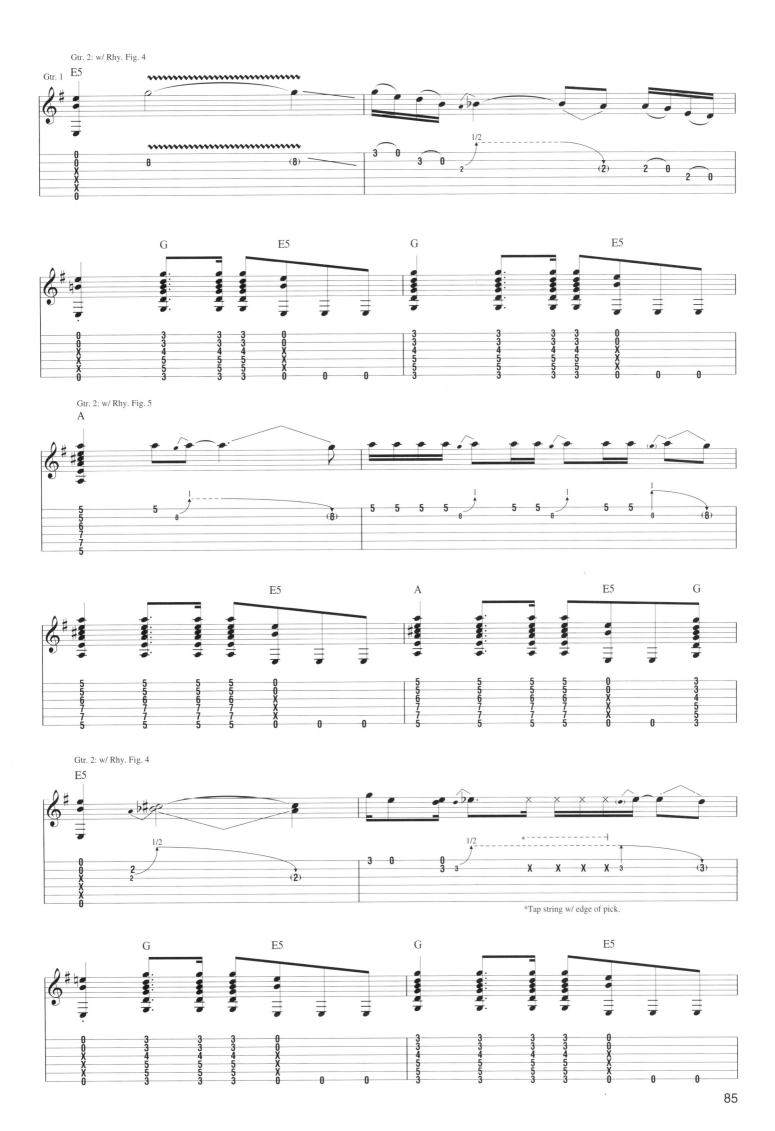

*Tap string w/ edge of pick.

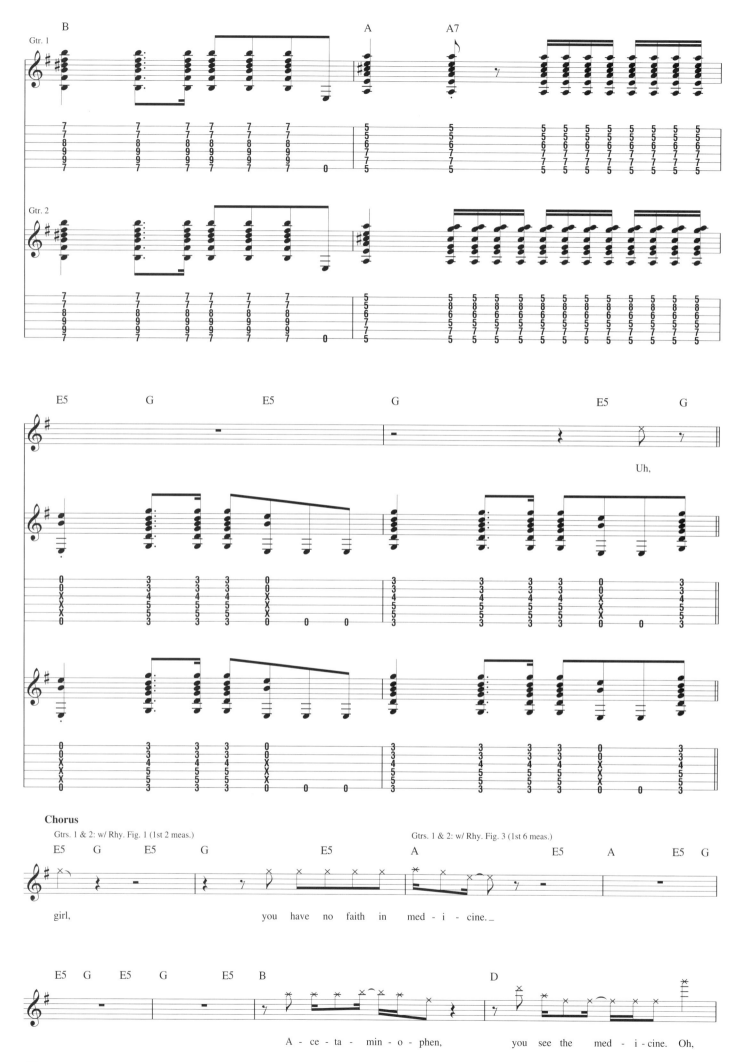

WELL IT'S TRUE THAT WE LOVE ONE ANOTHER

Words and Music by
Jack White

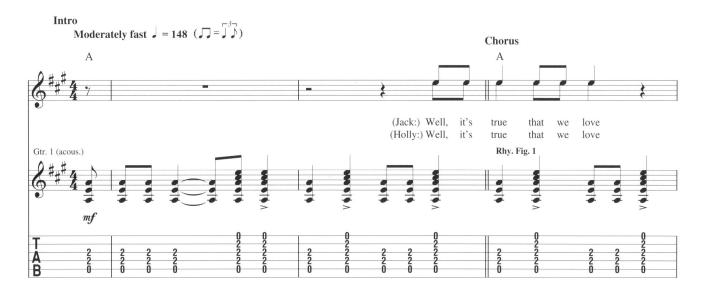

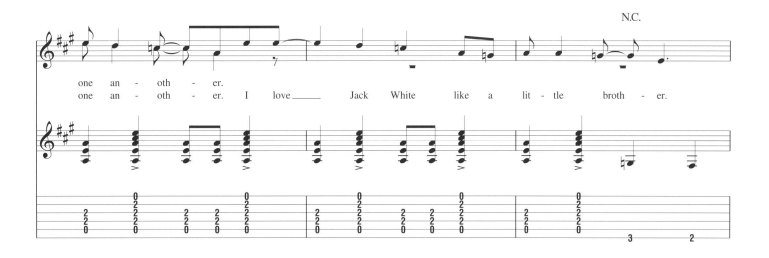

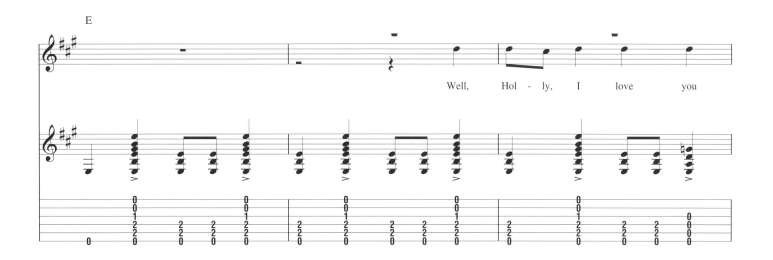

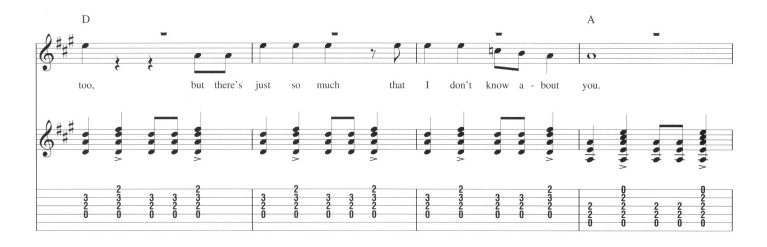

too, but there's just so much that I don't know a-bout you.

Verse

(Holly:) 1. Jack, give me some mon-ey to pay my bills.___ (Jack:) All the

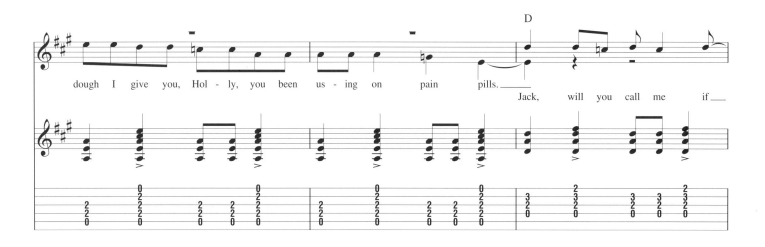

dough I give you, Hol-ly, you been us-ing on pain pills.___ Jack, will you call me if ___

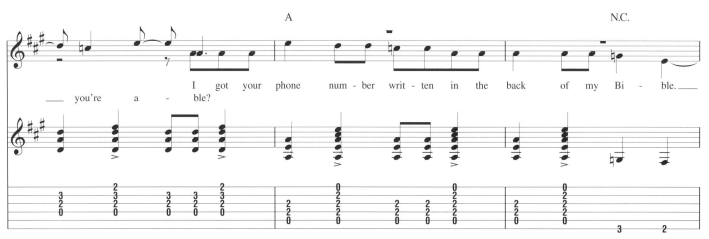

___ you're a - ble? I got your phone num-ber writ-ten in the back of my Bi-ble.___

Verse

Gtr. 1: w/ Rhy. Fig. 1

(Meg:) 3. Just say "Jack, do you a - dore me? (Jack:) Well,_____ I would, Hol - ly, but

love real - ly bores me._____ (Holly:) Then I

Then I

guess we should just be friends.

guess we should just be friends. I'm just kid - ding, Hol - ly. You

know that I'll love you till the end. (Jack:) Well, it's

(Holly:) Well, it's

Chorus

Gtr. 1: w/ Rhy. Fig. 1

true that we love one an - oth - er.

true that we love one an - oth - er. I love_____ Jack White like a

lit - tle broth - er. Well,

Hol - ly, I love you too, but there's just so much that

I don't know a - bout you. (Jack:) 4. Hol - ly,

Verse

Gtr. 1: w/ Rhy. Fig. 1 (1st 10 meas.)

give me some of your Eng - lish lov - in'.

(Holly:) If I did _____ that, Jack, _____ I'd have

one in the ov - en. Why don't you

go off and love your-self?

If I did that, Hol-ly, there

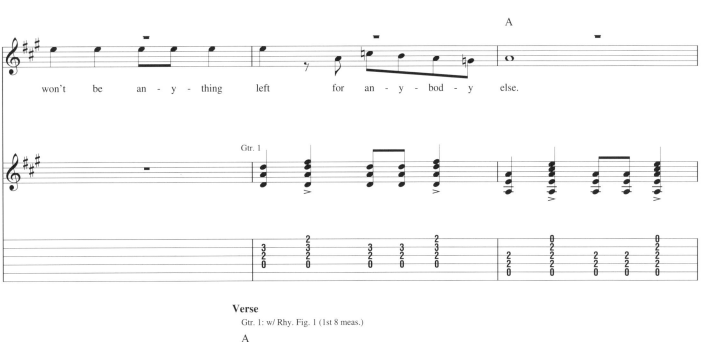

won't be an-y-thing left for an-y-bod-y else.

Verse
Gtr. 1: w/ Rhy. Fig. 1 (1st 8 meas.)

(Holly:) 5. Jack, it's too bad a-bout the way that you look.

(Jack:)You know I

gave that horse a car-rot so he'd break your foot.

(Meg:) Will the two of you cut it out,_____ and

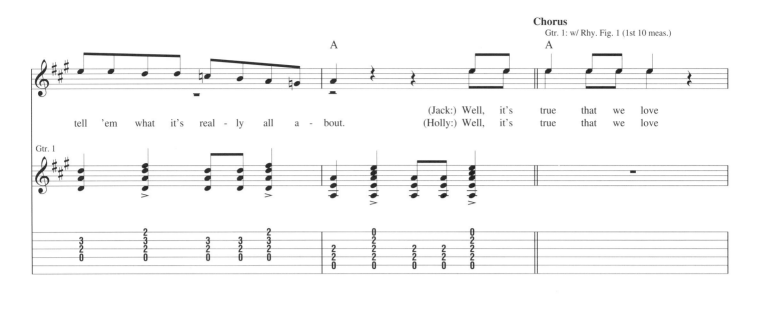

Chorus
Gtr. 1: w/ Rhy. Fig. 1 (1st 10 meas.)

(Jack:) Well, it's true that we love
(Holly:) Well, it's true that we love

tell 'em what it's real-ly all a - bout.

Gtr. 1

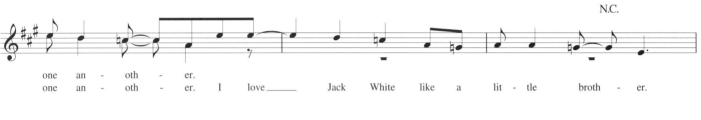

one an - oth - er.
one an - oth - er. I love_____ Jack White like a lit - tle broth - er.

Well, Hol - ly, I love you too, but there's

just so much that I _____ don't know a - bout

Gtr. 1

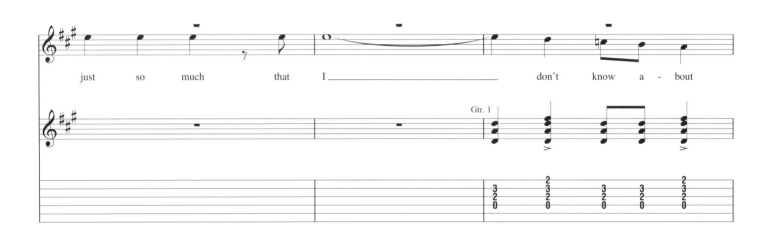

w/ studio chatter

you.

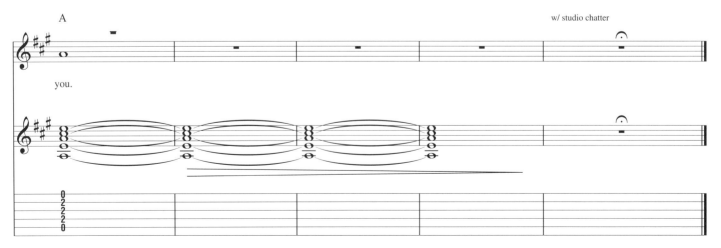

94

Guitar Notation Legend

Guitar Music can be notated three different ways: on a *musical staff*, in *tablature*, and in *rhythm slashes*.

RHYTHM SLASHES are written above the staff. Strum chords in the rhythm indicated. Use the chord diagrams found at the top of the first page of the transcription for the appropriate chord voicings. Round noteheads indicate single notes.

THE MUSICAL STAFF shows pitches and rhythms and is divided by bar lines into measures. Pitches are named after the first seven letters of the alphabet.

TABLATURE graphically represents the guitar fingerboard. Each horizontal line represents a string, and each number represents a fret.

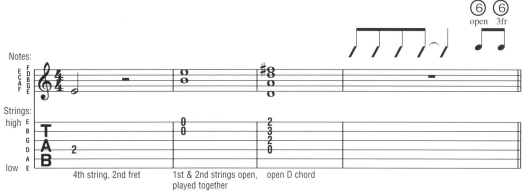

4th string, 2nd fret
1st & 2nd strings open, played together
open D chord

HALF-STEP BEND: Strike the note and bend up 1/2 step.

WHOLE-STEP BEND: Strike the note and bend up one step.

GRACE NOTE BEND: Strike the note and immediately bend up as indicated.

SLIGHT (MICROTONE) BEND: Strike the note and bend up 1/4 step.

BEND AND RELEASE: Strike the note and bend up as indicated, then release back to the original note. Only the first note is struck.

PRE-BEND: Bend the note as indicated, then strike it.

VIBRATO: The string is vibrated by rapidly bending and releasing the note with the fretting hand.

WIDE VIBRATO: The pitch is varied to a greater degree by vibrating with the fretting hand.

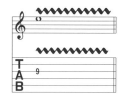

HAMMER-ON: Strike the first (lower) note with one finger, then sound the higher note (on the same string) with another finger by fretting it without picking.

PULL-OFF: Place both fingers on the notes to be sounded. Strike the first note and without picking, pull the finger off to sound the second (lower) note.

LEGATO SLIDE: Strike the first note and then slide the same fret-hand finger up or down to the second note. The second note is not struck.

SHIFT SLIDE: Same as legato slide, except the second note is struck.

TRILL: Very rapidly alternate between the notes indicated by continuously hammering on and pulling off.

TAPPING: Hammer ("tap") the fret indicated with the pick-hand index or middle finger and pull off to the note fretted by the fret hand.

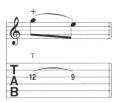

NATURAL HARMONIC: Strike the note while the fret-hand lightly touches the string directly over the fret indicated.

PINCH HARMONIC: The note is fretted normally and a harmonic is produced by adding the edge of the thumb or the tip of the index finger of the pick hand to the normal pick attack.

PICK SCRAPE: The edge of the pick is rubbed down (or up) the string, producing a scratchy sound.

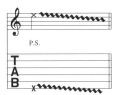

MUFFLED STRINGS: A percussive sound is produced by laying the fret hand across the string(s) without depressing, and striking them with the pick hand.

PALM MUTING: The note is partially muted by the pick hand lightly touching the string(s) just before the bridge.

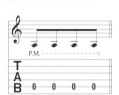

RAKE: Drag the pick across the strings indicated with a single motion.

TREMOLO PICKING: The note is picked as rapidly and continuously as possible.

VIBRATO BAR DIVE AND RETURN: The pitch of the note or chord is dropped a specified number of steps (in rhythm) then returned to the original pitch.

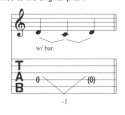

VIBRATO BAR SCOOP: Depress the bar just before striking the note, then quickly release the bar.

VIBRATO BAR DIP: Strike the note and then immediately drop a specified number of steps, then release back to the original pitch.

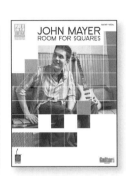